THE EFFECTS
OF PSYCHOTHERAPY

S. RACHMAN

Psychology Department,
Institute of Psychiatry, University of London

PERGAMON PRESS

OXFORD · NEW YORK · TORONTO
SYDNEY · BRAUNSCHWEIG

Pergamon Press Ltd., Headington Hill Hall, Oxford
Pergamon Press Inc., Maxwell House, Fairview Park, Elmsford,
New York 10523
Pergamon of Canada Ltd., 207 Queen's Quay West, Toronto 1
Pergamon Press (Aust.) Pty. Ltd., 19a Boundary Street,
Rushcutters Bay, N.S.W. 2011, Australia
Vieweg & Sohn GmbH, Burgplatz 1, Braunschweig

First edition 1971
Library of Congress Catalog Card No. 70–173763

Printed in Great Britain by A. Wheaton & Co , Exeter

08 016805 1 Hard cover
08 016807 8 Flexicover

INTERNATIONAL SERIES OF MONOGRAPHS IN
EXPERIMENTAL PSYCHOLOGY

GENERAL EDITOR: H. J. EYSENCK

VOLUME 15

THE EFFECTS OF PSYCHOTHERAPY

CONTENTS

CHAPTER 1

INTRODUCTION

PROFESSOR JEROME FRANK (1968) has observed that "we should not forget that, at least in the United States, psychiatrists and psychologists combined, treat far fewer persons than chiropractors and religious healers" (p. 39). A satisfactory explanation of the persistence of these types of practice might take us a long way in coming to grips with the effects of placebos and the array of psychotherapeutic procedures currently offered. Although Frank (1961) has provided an absorbing account of the common ground between faith healing, persuasion, and psychotherapy, the analogy should not be stretched. Unlike faith healing, psychotherapy is recommended and practised by professionals who have undergone scientific and critical training. This is not, however, a guarantee that its use is justified on scientific grounds. The rise and fall of insulin treatment is an instructive example of misguided therapy and serves as a useful reminder.

After a period of considerable popularity and widespread use in the treatment of schizophrenia, insulin coma therapy began to decline in the late fifties. Writing in 1959, Sargant gave a moderately favourable account of the treatment and stated that of 67 psychiatric hospitals in southern England, "every hospital except 1 private mental hospital and 2 neurosis centres in this area have been using Sakel's insulin coma treatment of schizophrenia during the last 10 years" (p. 148). A few years later Bennet (1966) reported that of 214 hospitals which had active insulin coma clinics in the 1950's, no less than 93 had discontinued these clinics. He also observed that insulin therapy and electro-shock had not altered hospital statistics—unlike the newer psychotropic drugs. After having endorsed insulin coma therapy in his well-known textbook, Kalinowsky (1967) wrote that "at present, insulin coma therapy is used

1

in very few places throughout the world". He felt that there was a need for this treatment, "perhaps 1 hospital in each area would be sufficient" (p. 1286). In his textbook published 15 years earlier (Kalinowsy and Hoch, 1952) he had stated that "acute cases of schizophrenia should have preference as it is an established fact that the chronic patient responds less well; but even in the chronic group there is a sufficient number of patients who show improvement and these should therefore not be excluded from treatment" (p. 12). Again, "insulin shock treatment was introduced for the cure of schizophrenia . . . in manic depressive psychoses and involutional psychoses, insulin is far less effective" (p. 11). Curran and Guttmann (1949, p. 158) observed that "the treatment of schizophrenia has been revolutionized by the introduction of shock therapy" (i.e. insulin shock and convulsive treatment). They recommended it as the treatment of first choice for schizophrenia and also stated that "it may be considered that insulin treatment should always be given in cases of recent origin and should be considered even in chronic cases . . . the better quality of the remission is one of the most striking effects of insulin therapy" (p. 160). In the following edition of their book (Curran and Partridge, 1955) their advice was more reserved: "although it can hardly be considered curative, it is the most effective way of treating schizophrenia that we have and the great majority of authorities agree that it produces remissions that are of better quality, are reached more quickly and last longer, than those obtainable by any other means" (p. 373). The next edition of the book appeared in 1963 and this time the pertinent paragraph quoted immediately above was deleted. Later, on the same page, the authors pointed out that insulin coma therapy "has been so largely replaced by the use of tranquilizers that details of the technique must be sought elsewhere" (p. 387).

These consecutive quotations illustrate the spectacular rise and fall of insulin coma treatment as seen by Curran and his colleagues. In the space of a mere 14 years—from 1949 to 1963—it changed from being a revolutionizing treatment to one which did not even merit description in a standard textbook.

Mayer-Gross *et al.* (1960) wrote in the second edition of their textbook that insulin coma treatment "is still recognized as one of the effective methods of treating early schizophrenia. If applied in the first year of the illness, it more than doubles the number of remissions that can be expected to occur" (p. 298). In the following edition, by Slater and Roth (1969), they pointed out that drugs have largely replaced insulin coma treatment, and the matter was dismissed in one sentence of an 800-page book. In the second edition published in 1960, the authors had remarked that "the empirical character of therapies such as insulin coma treatment has been the target of much criticism and an excuse for sceptical inertia" (p. 296). The third edition of the textbook contains a witty alteration in this sentence: "the empirical character of therapies such as ECT and pharmacological treatment has been the target of much criticism and an excuse for sceptical inertia" (p. 329).

In the 1947 edition of their textbook, Henderson and Gillespie were somewhat critical and reserved. Although they gave a detailed account of the treatment, they went on to say that "the efficacy of insulin coma treatment is still therefore somewhat difficult to estimate" (p. 404). And they added that there is a "suspicion that treatment with insulin, even if it is undertaken early, does not increase the ultimate rate of recovery" (p. 404). They seem to be justified (or better placed) in stating in their 1962 (Henderson and Batchelor) edition that "we are of the opinion that the treatment should be abandoned" (p. 347). They go on to add that "we have ceased to use insulin coma treatment and so have many others, some of whom were previously enthusiasts for the treatment" (p. 347). In a survey of 205 senior English psychiatrists published in 1965 (Willis and Bannister), only 6.8% regarded insulin coma as a suitable treatment for schizophrenia.

The story of insulin coma treatment is an interesting episode in the history of psychological medicine and would repay close analysis. It would be reassuring if we could believe that the abandonment of this method of treatment came as a direct consequence of a detached evaluation of scientific evidence. Although it is almost certainly true that evaluation of this type did play a role in the virtual disappearance of the treatment, the major cause for its decrease in popularity was probably the appearance of new and powerful tranquilizing drugs. We appear here to be dealing with a clear case of "treatment substitution". It has often been observed that theories (and techniques) seldom succumb to abstract argument: "theories pass from the scientific stage not because they have been disproved but because they have been superseded— pushed off and replaced by others that are new. I have searched long through the history of science without finding a single instance in which one could with any assurance say that criticism was the *coup de mort* of theory" (Dallenbach, 1955). Nevertheless, people are, of course, responsive to argument and evidence. Criticism can often provoke further thoughts and a search for supporting evidence. It can also promote a vigorous search for satisfactory alternatives. The fact that some critics expressed their doubts and reservations about insulin coma treatment probably facilitated the transition to tranquilizing drugs.

Even though psychotherapy today probably has more advocates than critics, there is a growing recognition and acknowledgement of the fact that supporting evidence is scarce. The main purpose of this book is to examine the nature and quality of the evidence, but a few remarks about the possible reasons for the uncritical and seemingly over-optimistic attitude towards psychotherapy will not be out of place.

Both patients and therapists can over-estimate the effects of treatment. For example, Feifel and Eells (1963) asked patients and therapists to assess the same psychotherapy and found large differences in their evaluations. Sixty-three patients and 28 therapists gave their views on the relative frequency of change after treatment. On symptom relief, only 27% of the patients claimed benefit, whereas 57% of the therapists felt that significant symptom-relief had been obtained. On the behavioural assessment, 47% of patients claimed improvements, whereas 71% of therapists reported improvements. In both cases there was a statistically significant difference between the reports of the patients and their therapists—with the therapists claiming far more improvement than their patients. In the famous Cambridge Somerville study on the prevention of delinquency, both the clients and the therapists reported far more benefit than was observed in the hard factual information about offences and court appearances (Teuber and Powers, 1953). The literature on placebo reactions is replete with examples of reported improvements after the administration of inert substances (e.g. Koegler and Brill, 1967, who found that 52% of their neurotic patients claimed such benefits). In the growing literature on behaviour therapy, similar instances of "mistaken" impressions are emerging. In his experimental treatment of fear of public speaking in a college population, Paul (1966) found that a significant minority of his subjects in a control group who received a nonsensical form of treatment (described as "attention placebo") felt that they had benefited from the experience. In the study by Lang *et al.* (1966) a group of snake-phobic students who had been given a meaningless form of talking pseudo-therapy also reported that they felt benefited—despite the fact that their fears were unaltered. In a recently completed clinical trial, Gillan (1971) found that psychotherapists consistently overrated the effects of treatment in comparison with their patients. This list of examples could be extended.

The major point is no longer in dispute. There are many non-specific elements in almost all forms of treatment which have apparently beneficial results. This built-in inflation effect, combined with the natural spontaneous remission which takes place in many psychological disorders, makes it extremely difficult to isolate the specific contribution made by any therapeutic technique. These scientific obstacles increase the fascination of the problem and can be moderately well tolerated as both of these processes operate in a manner which is desirable as far as the patients are concerned. It may turn out, in the long run, that psychotherapy does no more than provide the patient with a degree of comfort while the disorder runs its natural course. If this is so, then the sooner we establish such a finding the sooner we will be in a position honestly to provide effective comfort.

Although doubts about the effectiveness of psychotherapy had been expressed before the publication of their important findings, Teuber and Powers (1953) argued convincingly that the burden of proof lay with those who practise or advocate psychotherapy. In 1952 Eysenck published his now-famous evaluation of the effects of psychotherapy and concluded that the case was not proven. This important contribution is the starting point for most critiques of psychotherapy and, with his expanded assessment published in 1960, will be described first.

The focus of interest in Eysenck's work and in the present book is on *outcome* studies. The technical problems involved in such studies are of secondary concern, and an extensive literature on this subject is available (e.g. successive issues of the *International Journal of Psychiatry*, February and March of 1969; the *Annual Reviews of Psychology* over the past 15 years, etc.). Unless otherwise specified, "psychotherapy" is intended to mean *interpretive therapy* and *not* the support, reassurance, encouragement, guidance, and sympathetic listening which still form the mainstay of psychiatric practice. My reason for concentrating on interpretive types of therapy is that the most important and far-reaching claims have been made for this method. They are said to offer important benefits in excess of those provided by "superficial" types of psychotherapy and also to be capable of helping patients who would otherwise remain beyond treatment.

CHAPTER 2

EYSENCK'S ARGUMENT

LANDIS (1937), Denker (1946), and Zubin (1953)—among others—had questioned the claims made on behalf of psychotherapy and other forms of treatment prior to the appearance of Eysenck's classic paper of 1952. Prompted partly by their views, Eysenck carried out an astringent examination of the evidence on the effects of psychotherapy and came to the conclusion that the emperor had no clothes. The reactions of shock and disbelief have passed over and now, 19 years later, the time is suitable for a re-examination of the emperor's sartorial progress.

In this brief recapitulation I have attempted to extract the most salient points from Eysenck's argument as presented in 1952 and extended in 1960 and 1969. In his first evaluation he pointed out that an accurate assessment of psychotherapeutic effects is impeded by the methodological shortcomings found in most studies. In the absence of suitable control studies he had to rely on non-controlled studies and, as he noted, this precludes any definitive conclusions. In an attempt to provide a baseline with which to compare the results of treatment conducted without controls, he attempted to derive a "best available estimate" of remissions which occur in the absence of therapy. Recognizing the difficulty of this task, he pointed out the obvious defects involved in an attempt of this kind. The matching of cases is difficult, the cases are inadequately described, the nature and severity of the illnesses are not given in unequivocal detail, the data on duration and type of treatment are inadequate, and follow-up information is scanty. For these reasons he cautioned that his actuarial evaluations should not be regarded as providing precise comparisons.

Using the data provided by Landis and by Denker, his first estimate of the crude spontaneous remission rate in neurotic disorders led him to propose that approximately 2 out of 3 patients can be expected to recover within 2 years—even in the absence of formal treatment. In his second evaluation, Eysenck (1960a) supplemented this baseline with data provided by Shepherd and Gruenberg (1957). They attempted to estimate the duration of neurotic illnesses by reference to the general rule that "the prevalence of an illness in a population is equal to the product of its incidence and duration". In their data they observed that the incidence and prevalence curves for neurotic illnesses were of similar shape and ran an almost parallel course. From this they concluded that the average duration of neurotic illnesses is between 1 and 2 years. These authors summed up their study as follows: "While it is well known that neurotic illnesses can occur at any age and exhibit extremely long courses as well as very brief courses, the available data are remarkably consistent in suggesting that neurotic illnesses are not characteristic of early adult life, that there is a rising incidence and prevalence during the twenties and thirties, a parallel rising prevalence continuing into the forties, and then a rapid decline in prevalence of recognized neuroses. From these data it is perfectly clear that, in the mass, neuroses must have a limited course even if untreated; in fact, the best available data would suggest an average duration of between 1 and 2 years."

This conclusion, published 5 years after Eysenck's original article, was, of course, even more optimistic than his estimate. As Eysenck's initial estimate was based on the data provided by Landis and by Denker, a brief description of their work is necessary. Landis examined the amelioration rate in state mental hospitals for patients classified under the heading of "neurosis". He observed that in New York State, 70% of neurotic patients were discharged annually as recovered or improved. For the United States as a whole, the figure was 68%. Because of the obvious difficulties involved in an estimate of this kind (e.g. the patients must have been severely disturbed in order to require admission, some of them may well have received some psychotherapy, etc.), Landis was cautious in his conclusion: "Although this is not, strictly speaking, a basic figure for 'spontaneous' recovery, still any therapeutic method must show an appreciably greater size than this to be seriously considered."

Denker's (1946) baseline of spontaneous remission was calculated from 500 consecutive patients with disability claims due to neurosis who were treated by general practitioners. In no case was anything more than the most superficial type of psychotherapy employed, but sedatives, reassurance, and suggestion played a regular part in the treatment. These cases were followed up for a minimum of 5 years and often as long as 10 years after the period of disability had begun, and reasonably strict criteria of improvement were used. Denker found that 45% of these patients recovered within a year and an additional 27% after 2 years. The combined figure of 72% recoveries within 2 years increased during the course of the next 3 years and reached an eventual total of 90% recoveries after 5 years.

While recognizing the defects of these two studies, Eysenck was nevertheless struck by the extent of similarity between them—despite the fact that they were dealing with very different populations. He also fitted an exponential curve to the data (Fig. 1) which illustrates the natural course of neuroses. These necessarily gross estimates have now been supplemented by small-scale studies including experimental investigations. On the whole, as will be seen in Chapter 3, the initial crude estimates have received a reasonable measure of support.

Having established a rough baseline, Eysenck compared the rate of improvement reported in treated case series with the spontaneous remission baseline.

In his first evaluation he selected 24 of the most informative studies, covering over 7000 cases. Five of the reports described the results of psychoanalytic treatment. The results from the various studies were analysed into 4 categories of improvement ranging from cured or much improved to unimproved. In light of the variations between reports, Eysenck often had to use his judgement in determining some of the classifications of improvement and diagnostic groupings (an attempt was made to exclude all non-neurotic cases). He acknowledged that a "slight degree of subjectivity inevitably enters into this procedure, but it is doubtful if it has caused much distortion". His calculations based on these figures led him to conclude that "patients treated by means of psychoanalysis improved to the extent of 44%; patients treated eclectically improved to the extent of 64%; patients treated only custodially or by general practitioners improved to the extent of 72%. There thus appears to be an inverse correlation between recovery and psychotherapy", but this last conclusion "requires certain qualification". The

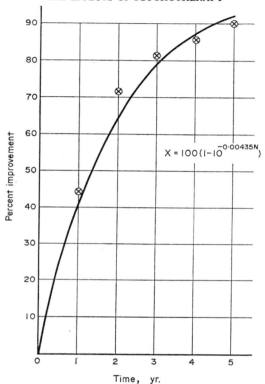

FIG. 1. Curve fitted to Denker's data on 500 untreated neurotic patients (Eysenck, 1960a). Improvement shown by 500 severe neurotics not receiving psychotherapy after between 1 and 5 years. In the formula X denotes the proportional improvement, while N denotes the number of weeks elapsing from the beginning of the experiment.

main qualification is that, if one excludes patients who break off psychoanalytic treatment before the therapist feels that it should be concluded, then the recovery rate with this form of treatment rises to 66%. That is, if one excluded the defectors, the chances of improvement with psychoanalytic treatment are approximately equal to the chances of improvement under eclectic treatment.

Having pointed out the obvious shortcomings in actuarial comparisons of the type which he had undertaken, Eysenck stated his provoking and now famous conclusion: "They fail to prove that psychotherapy, Freudian or otherwise, facilitates the recovery of neurotic patients. They show that roughly two-thirds of a group of neurotic patients will recover or improve to a marked extent within about 2 years of the onset of their illness, whether they are treated by means of psychotherapy or not."

In his re-examination of the evidence carried out 8 years later, Eysenck included a number of studies which had employed control groups. He gave "pride of place" to the Cambridge Somerville study on the prevention of delinquency. Teuber and Powers (1953) attempted, over a period of 8 years, to prevent delinquency by guidance, counselling, and therapy in a group of 650 underprivileged boys who had been designated as likely to become delinquent. Half of the boys were randomly allocated to the treatment group and the other half served as controls. The treatment consisted of individual therapy, and the majority of the therapists were either psychoanalytic or non-directive in orientation. As it was a complex study and the results are extensive, I will merely draw attention to the main findings. According to the authors, the "treatment did not . . . reduce the incidence of adjudged delinquency in the treatment group"; this despite the fact that the therapists felt that more than two-thirds of their sample had "substantially benefited". Similarly, 62% of the treated clients stated that the help provided had been of value to them. Despite these feelings of success and optimism, the objective evidence was "paradoxical", for the authors found that "instead of confirming the expectation that the treatment group would be less delinquent than the matched control group, there is a slight difference in favour of the control group". Teuber and Powers placed greater weight on the "quantitative indices" and concluded that "the data yield one definite conclusion: that the burden of proof is on anyone who claims specific results for a given form of therapy".

In the next study, 150 neurotic patients were tested on the MMPI before and after therapy (Barron and Leary, 1955). However, 23 of the patients had to wait an average of 7 months before treatment could commence, and they served as a waiting control group. Twenty-four comparisons were made between the treated and control groups and only one of them, the K score, was significant. This change is, as the authors agree, difficult to interpret, whereas on the "neurotic triad" (depression, psychasthenia, and hypochondriasis scales) "the average decrease is slightly greater for the controls than for the group therapy patients". If one could allow that the MMPI is a satisfactory measure of psychiatric improvement, which is doubtful, then the study was a complete failure to demonstrate the effectiveness of psychotherapy (in this case predominantly psychoanalytic in orientation). Barron and Leary attempted to salvage some comfort from the study by arguing that a commitment to undertake psychotherapy in the future and the initial contact with the clinic were themselves therapeutic events. Although this seems to be stretching the point somewhat, their claim is not wholly unreasonable. The fact remains, however, that their study failed to demonstrate that psychotherapy facilitated the improvement of this group of patients.

The Rogers and Dymond (1954) study of the effects of non-directive therapy employed a double control group technique. Some of the treated patients acted as their own controls by undergoing a 60-day waiting period before commencing therapy. In addition to the 29 treated cases, 23 "normal volunteers" acted as a further control. The authors claimed to have demonstrated a significant therapeutic effect, but Eysenck's 3 main criticisms are telling. In the first place, the use of normal subjects as a control group for patients is unsupportable: "no one has, to our knowledge, advanced the hypothesis that a group of normal people not subjected to any kind of psychotherapeutic or other manipulation should change in the direction of greater integration and better mental health" (Eysenck, 1960a, p. 707). In regard to the waiting control procedure, he pointed out that the time intervals were not comparable. The waiting period was only 60 days, and it is improbable that much spontaneous remission would have occurred during this short period. As the therapy period was apparently of greater duration, the possibility of spontaneous changes occurring during *this* period was enhanced. Lastly, Eysenck drew attention to the absence of any behavioural criteria of outcome. He might also have added that the use of the Q-sort was perhaps unwise (see Chapter 5).

The Brill and Beebe (1955) study is a statistical analysis of data collected on military patients. In a highly detailed analysis of substantial data they found that treatment had no apparent effect on the patient's condition after discharge, nor on the percentage of soldiers who were considered fit to return to duty. Although the authors searched long and hard, they were unable to find evidence to support the claim that psychotherapy had been effective in the treatment of these patients. Despite its retrospective quality, this study is impressive in the care and effort taken to collect, sort, and interpret the evidence. As far as the argument for psychotherapy is concerned, it brings cold comfort. The study reported by Ellis (1957), which compares the effects of three types of therapy, suffers from serious defects but is not without interest. He compared the results obtained with 78 patients treated with his own brand of "rational psychotherapy", 78 patients treated by psycho-analytic-oriented psychotherapy, and 16 who received orthodox psychoanalysis. The patients were all treated by Ellis himself, who also carried out the assessments of outcome (an unwise undertaking). Nevertheless, he found that 90% of the group who received rational therapy improved whereas only 63% of the analytic group showed a similar degree of improvement. Of the 16 patients who received ortho-dox psychoanalysis, only 50% showed the same degree of improvement. The 2 other studies described at some length by Eysenck (Wolpe and Lakin Phillips) are discussed in Chapters 10 and 8 respectively.

This necessarily abbreviated account of Eysenck's (1960a) evidence and argument is best concluded by stating its 8 major conclusions, which, as he pointed out, go "a little beyond those" of the original survey. The major shift is towards increasing pessimism about psycho-therapy—a move from "unproven" to "unlikely". The conclusions are:

"1. When untreated neurotic control groups are compared with experimental groups of neurotic patients treated by means of psychotherapy, both groups recover to approximately the same extent.

2. When soldiers who have suffered a neurotic breakdown and have not received psychotherapy are compared with soldiers who have received psychotherapy, the chances of the two groups returning to duty are approximately equal.

3. When neurotic soldiers are separated from the service, their chances of recovery are not affected by their receiving or not receiving psychotherapy.

4. Civilian neurotics who are treated by psychotherapy recover or

improve to approximately the same extent as similar neurotics receiving no psychotherapy.

5. Children suffering from emotional disorders and treated by psychotherapy recover or improve to approximately the same extent as similar children not receiving psychotherapy.

6. Neurotic patients treated by means of psychotherapeutic procedures based on learning theory improve significantly more quickly than do patients treated by means of psychoanalysis or electric psychotherapy, or not treated by psychotherapy at all.

7. Neurotic patients treated by psychoanalytic psychotherapy do not improve more quickly than patients treated by means of eclectic psychotherapy, and may improve less quickly when account is taken of the large proportion of patients breaking off treatment.

8. With the single exception of psychotherapeutic methods based on learning theory, results of published research with military and civilian neurotics, and with both adults and children, suggest that the therapeutic effects of psychotherapy are small or non-existent, and do not in any demonstrable way add to the non-specific effects of routine medical treatment, or to such events as occur in patients' every-day experience."

Some of the conclusions included in this list (e.g. psychotherapy with children) are discussed in subsequent chapters.

Naturally, Eysenck's arguments have not gone unchallenged. A great deal of discussion and research has been generated by these two contributions, and many writers have debated these matters at some length, despite Sanford's (1953) advice*: "the only wise course with respect to such a challenge is to ignore it." In the event it was Sanford's advice which was ignored. The views expressed range from outright rejection to ready acceptance of Eysenck's assessment.

---

* The view that a statistical examination of the effects of psychoanalysis is unwise and/or unnecessary still has adherents; some of them may enjoy a fellow feeling with Freud, who wrote: "Friends of analysis have advised us to counterbalance a collection of failures by drawing up a statistical enumeration of successes. I have not taken up this suggestion either. I brought forward the argument that statistics would be valueless if the units collated were not alike, and the cases which had been treated were in fact not equivalent in many respects. Further, the period of time that could be reviewed was too short for one to be able to judge of the permanence of the cures; and of many cases it would be impossible to give any account" (Freud, 1922).

Arguing that the entire question is "scientifically meaningless", Sanford stated his view in a manner which was, despite his assertion, something less than obvious. He stated that "it is obvious that some people change in some ways under the influence of some kinds of therapeutic activities while other people do not change, or change in different ways, under the same therapeutic activity, and that still other people change in ways similar to the above without any therapeutic activity" (p. 336). Not very enlightening.

Numerous writers have, of course, drawn attention to the limitations of the data on which Eysenck's evaluation was based (many of the problems were in fact mentioned by Eysenck in his original paper). Rosenzweig (1954), for example, drew attention to the difficulties involved in comparing outcome criteria across different studies. Although Eysenck discussed this problem in a slightly different form, the conclusion drawn by Rosenzweig in his argument is somewhat different but not uncharacteristic. Having discussed the shortcomings of the data, he argued that the criticisms of psychotherapy were not crucial and that they do not prove that psychotherapy is ineffective. This point of view has in fact been adopted by several people, but it appears to miss the main issue. As Teuber and Powers (1953) remarked in their discussion of the Cambridge study, the burden of proof rests with those who recommend or practise psychotherapy and *not* with those who persist in reminding us that the evidence in support of the beneficial effects of psychotherapy is embarrassingly scanty.

A good deal of the discussion provoked by Eysenck's work has, however, been productive and provoking. Meehl (1955), for example, discusses the problem in an extremely thoughtful manner. Malan *et al.* (1968), accepting that "the case for a high rate of symptomatic remission in neurotic patients . . . is proved and that is the end of it", made an interesting attempt to study the psychodynamic changes which occur in untreated neurotic patients. Their study, based on a 2- to 8-year follow-up of 45 untreated Tavistock Clinic patients, showed that 51% were "at least symptomatically improved", but they also argued that a proportion of these changes were "psychodynamically suspect". The value of this type of investigation, attempted in part in response to Eysenck's analysis, is beyond question, but the methods adopted are, unfortunately, unsatisfactory. The main difficulty arises from their mixture of interpretation with factual evidence. Despite this methodologica drawback, their investigation is of considerable interest and will, one hopes, prompt further improved studies of this kind.

Another advance in our knowledge which must be attributed, indirectly, to Eysenck's analysis is the recognition that future studies of remissions (both spontaneous and treated) will be more precise and valuable if they are carried out within rather than across diagnostic groupings. The emphasis on this point arises from Eisenberg's response to the evaluation of the effects of psychotherapy with children which Levitt published in 1957 (see Chapter 8).

One of the most interesting developments to flow from Eysenck's argument is the concept of "average therapeutic effects". This, in turn, has given added impetus to those research workers engaged in the study of effective therapist variables, with particular reference to non-directive therapy (see Chapter 7). Bergin (1966) has been one of the most articulate advocates of the "average therapeutic effect" argument. His attempt at an optimistic reconciliation of the predominantly dis-appointing evidence on the effects of psychotherapy is so astute that it deserves success. Unfortunately, as is shown in Chapter 7, it would be too successful if it were correct and, as it turns out, the facts are against it. He argues that while reports and studies show little difference in the average amount of change occurring after treatment, a "significant increase in the variability of criterion scores appears at post-testing in the treatment groups". This spread of criterion scores, he argues, implies that treatment has a beneficial effect on some patients and an unfavour-able effect on others. "When these contrary phenomena are lumped together in an experimental group, they cancel each other out to some extent and the overall yield in terms of improvement . . . is no greater than the change occurring in a control group."

Like Bergin, Truax and Carkhuff (1967) in their important book accept the argument based on an average therapeutic effect and from that point extend their search for the variables which determine success-ful or unsuccessful treatment outcomes. On average, psychotherapy appears to be ineffective. If we assume, however, that treated groups show increased variability at termination, then we need to isolate those factors which improve some patients and make others worse. While allowing for the influence of other determinants, Truax and Carkhuff and their colleagues have devoted most of their attention to an examination of the characteristics of successful and unsuccessful therapists. This line of argument and the associated research are encouraging examples of the fruitful effects which can emerge from a critical, if unpopular, examination of a prevailing belief.

Eysenck (1960a, 1969a) has discussed many of these problems in developments of his original argument and reiterated his view that the proof of psychotherapeutic effectiveness rests with those who advocate it: "psychoanalysts and psychotherapists generally assert that their methods cure psychoneurotic disorders, and are in fact the only methods which can achieve this end. Clearly, therefore, it is on them that the onus of proof must rest" (Eysenck, 1969a). He goes on to say that "they must define clearly and unambiguously what is meant by neurotic disorder and what is meant by cure; they must put forward methods of testing the effects of the treatment which are not dependent on the subjective evaluation of the therapist, and they must demonstrate that their methods give results which are clearly superior to any alternative methods, such as those of behaviour therapy or of spontaneous remission. It is indisputable, I suggest, that psychotherapists and psychoanalysts have failed to do any of these things, and until they have all been done I find it very difficult to see how any doubt can be thrown on my conclusion that published research has failed to support the claims made" (p. 100). Acknowledging the limitations of actuarial and similar types of information, he went on to urge "the necessity of properly planned and executed experimental studies into this important field" with recommendations about the manner in which such studies might be conducted.

Shortly after the publication of his 1952 review, Eysenck became interested in the possibility of developing an alternative to psychotherapy. During the past 10 years he has advocated the development of behavioural therapy, the progress of which is discussed in Chapter 10. "We are not, therefore, faced with the alternative . . . of psychotherapy or nothing; we are in the position of having two contenders in the ring between whom a rational choice should not be impossible" (Eysenck, 1969a, p. 99).

This, then, is the background to the debate about psychotherapy which is the subject of this book.

CHAPTER 3

SPONTANEOUS REMISSIONS
IN NEUROTIC DISORDERS

RECOGNITION that the majority of neurotic disorders can be expected to remit within 2 years in the absence of formal psychiatric treatment is the first step in what will undoubtedly prove to be a long and complex process of investigation. Many people have already recommended that we now focus attention on the remission rates which occur in different diagnostic categories, and there can be little argument that this is a necessary and inevitable development. We already have many indications of the variation which occurs between diagnostic groupings, but a systematic analysis has yet to be conducted. Some other interesting problems which have emerged from a recognition of the occurrence of spontaneous remissions also merit attention. Every investigation reported so far has produced evidence of a group of patients who fail to remit spontaneously—the figures range from 20% to as high as 50%—and we need to identify and describe these persisting disorders with accuracy. We also need to investigate the reasons why these disorders persist and, indeed, show deterioration in a number of cases. Another important problem which will require some explanation arises from the observation that *treated* patients rarely show an improvement rate in excess of the spontaneous remission rate. On occasions, treated patients seem to show an improvement rate which is lower than that of the spontaneous remission rate. Even if we allow for the likelihood that therapy may make some patients worse, it seems most improbable that a large discrepancy between treated improvement rates and spontaneous improvement rates can be accounted for satisfactorily in this manner. The large discrepancies which have been recorded may be attributable to the selection of unrepresentative samples of patients for inclusion in certain treatment series. For example, if a treatment series includes a disproportionately large number of "hard-core" patients, then the improvement rate may well fail to reach the spontaneous improvement rate of two-thirds. A second factor which may contribute to treated improvement rates which fall below the spontaneous-rate figure is the duration of treatment and follow-up (where applicable). If the treatment period is relatively brief, then the outcome figures may again fall below those of the spontaneous improvement rate, which is usually quoted in terms of a 2-year period.

Some interesting pointers which may facilitate investigations into the nature of remissions (spontaneous or treated) are provided in a monograph by Greer and Cawley (1966), who carried out a 4- to 6-year follow-up investigation of 160 neurotic patients who were admitted to the Maudsley Hospital and many of whom received psychotherapy. The investigation was extensive and thorough, and only certain findings can be mentioned here. One of their conclusions was that "2 of the principal prognostic indicators in neurotic illness are pre-morbid personality and the nature of the illness" (p. 88). These indicators were not necessarily related to each other. In regard to diagnostic groupings they found that patients with depressive, hysterical, or anxiety reactions had the most favourable outcomes, while those with obsessive compulsive or hypochondriacal symptoms had a poor prognosis. Patients with obsessive reactions were found to have the longest duration of symptoms and depressive patients to have the shortest duration. Patients with anxiety and hysterical reactions had illness durations of moderate length. These findings lead to the suggestion that the obsessional and hypochondriacal patients may constitute a disproportionate number of the hard-core patients. Prognosis was related to a number of variables describing pre-morbid personality and precipitating events.

The variables found to be "significantly associated with a favourable prognosis include: (a) married civil status; (b) normal pre-morbid personality; (c) satisfactory pre-morbid social adjustment with respect to work record, inter-personal relations and marital relations; (d) evidence of precipitating factors preceding the onset of illness; (e) less than 5 years' duration of symptoms; (f) presence of depressive symptoms and absence of disorders of thought content—in particular hypochondriacal preoccupations; (g) a diagnosis of depressive or hysterical reactions; (h) . . . patient lives in a domestic group the members of which show a sympathetic and tolerant attitude towards him . . . ". Some of the main variables found to be associated with an unfavourable prognosis included disturbed pre-morbid personality, unsatisfactory interpersonal relations, unsatisfactory work record, absence of precipitating factors, duration of more than 5 years, disorders of thought content. Equally interesting are some of the variables which appeared, in this study at least, to have no significant relationship to outcome in neurotic disorders. They include: "age, sex, social class, family history, childhood environment, neurotic traits in childhood, intelligence, premorbid sexual adjustment, a history of previous psychiatric illness, length of stay in hospital, presence or absence of associated organic disease, material circumstances after discharge from hospital, and occurrence of stressful events since discharge" (p. 88).

The findings reported in this study are of considerable potential value provided they are used with care. Firstly, it is likely that the sample is in certain respects atypical. It probably contained a disproportionately large number of severe cases and, in addition, the Maudsley Hospital is a major teaching institution and in this sense uncharacteristic. Nevertheless, the monograph can be used as a sound and convenient starting point for further studies.

I will not attempt a premature estimation of the spontaneous remission rates which might be expected to occur in various diagnostic groups or how these rates might relate to particular patient variables. However, on the basis of the Greer–Cawley study, the work of Marks (1969), much anecdotal evidence found in the studies referred to in this chapter and also on the basis of clinical observations, it is possible to risk certain speculations of a general character. We can predict that the league table for spontaneous remissions in different disorders may look something like this (in descending order): affective neurotic disorders, anxiety states, hysterical disorders, obsessional illnesses, sexual disorders other than homosexuality, hypochondriacal disorders. Circumscribed phobias present in patients over the age of approximately 15 years will probably feature low in the table, but other types of phobic disorder will probably be close to the rate obtaining in anxiety states.

Variables other than diagnostic category must also be taken into account as spontaneous remissions are neither complete nor wholly absent in any of the diagnostic groupings. The nature of these other contributing factors has been alluded to in discussing the Greer–Cawley study and no doubt will be elaborated in time. Even though they found a clear relationship between long-term duration of the disorder and poor prognosis, we can anticipate certain matters which will be dealt with later in this chapter by saying that the relationship between long-term duration and poor prognosis does not obtain in certain forms of treatment. This is demonstrated most clearly in the treatment of circumscribed phobias which, even though they probably have a low spontaneous remission rate, respond well and promptly to desensitization.

Global estimates of remission can be supplemented by a number of reports and investigations carried out on smaller samples of untreated patients. Wallace and Whyte (1959) reported on the progress made by "83 psychoneurotic patients who had been promised psychotherapy and who failed to receive it" because of an absence of adequate facilities. The patients were followed up 3–7 years later and valid information was obtained on 49 of them. The overall spontaneous improvement rate was 65.3% and the improvement rate for each diagnostic group was: anxiety state 68%, hysteria 50%, miscellaneous 75%. Seven patients who had obtained treatment in the interim were excluded from the analysis. Wallace and Whyte found that those patients who had recovered tended to have more stable marriages and more satisfactory group relationships than those who failed to recover. They also found evidence that any spontaneous improvements which take place tend to occur within the first 3 years. Wallace and Whyte could detect no significant differences in respect of recovery and diagnosis between those who failed to reply initially and those who did reply. Although the overall spontaneous remission rate accords well with the gross estimate described earlier, this report is, of course, based on a small population. Nevertheless, the finding that patients with different diagnoses show different rates of improvement is important.

A similar type of study was reported by Saslow and Peters (1956). They followed up 83 patients who had been considered suitable for treatment but had not received it. The follow-ups were conducted by post or by interview and occurred from 1 to 6 years after notification.

Regrettably they provide no indication of a possible relationship between extent of improvement and the follow-up time which had elapsed. It is, of course, likely that there would be differences in the estimates provided at a year after notification and at 6 years after notification. Despite some flaws in their procedure, Saslow's and Peters's study did produce interesting data, and their overall spontaneous remission-rate figure is lower than usual. They found that "37% were found significantly improved". If we exclude from this overall rate the 16% who were diagnosed as schizophrenic and the 4% "mental deficiency", then the remission figure would be inflated—this is implied but not stated in their discussion. Even so, the figures are lower than usual. In addition to the reasons already suggested, it is possible that their findings can be accounted for by the inclusion of a surprisingly high proportion of patients with hysteria—30%. Most of these patients had a poor outcome, and while this observation is in keeping with that reported by Wallace and Whyte whose patients with hysteria showed a lower spontaneous remission rate than the rest of the sample, it is not consistent with the Greer–Cawley results.

Schorer *et al.* (1968) traced 138 patients who had been placed on a waiting list for psychotherapy, and of these 55 (39%) were found to have received no treatment in the follow-up period, which averaged 5 years. The spontaneous remission rate for these untreated patients, comprising neurotics and people with personality disorders, was 65% ("proved to be definitely improved"). These improvements were widespread and included increased social effectiveness as well as significant changes in the presenting complaints. A group of 41 patients who obtained treatment elsewhere "were found to be 78% improved—not significantly more than those who improved without treatment". The authors comment on the similarity of their results to those reported by Wallace and Whyte (1959) but could detect "little predictability about who would improve without treatment and who would not".

In an exceptionally long-term follow-up (averaging 24 years) of 120 neurotics who had received little or no specific treatment, 93 (i.e. 77%) were found to be much improved (Ernst, 1959). More recently, in an actuarial study of 5 New York clinics where the main method of treatment is psychotherapy, Saluger reported a spontaneous remission rate of 55% in 1 year. The untreated| patients were compared with the treated ones on 16 variables and only one small difference emerged at follow-up. The rates of improvement on a variety of indices were all in the 50–60% range, and the rates for treated and untreated patients were almost identical.

An original and interesting study of patients attending the psycho-analytic Tavistock Clinic was described by Malan *et al.* (1968). Starting with the view that the case for a high rate of symptomatic remission in neurotic patients is proved, they attempted to discover the psycho-dynamic changes which occur in untreated patients. Their case material is absorbing, but unfortunately the conclusions they reach are blurred by a mixture of fact and interpretation. The reports are open to other, simpler explanations, which need make no psychodynamic assumptions and which would, of course, lead to different conclusions. Nonetheless, the bald findings in this 2- to 8-year follow-up of 45 untreated patients were that 51% "were found to be symptomatically improved" but a minority of these were "psychodynamically suspect". There can be little doubt, however, that if a similar examination were made of treated cases, a proportion of them would also be regarded as suspect. An extension of this work along two lines would seem to be worth while. Judges could be asked to rate treated and untreated cases in ignorance of the therapeutic actions recommended or instituted. In addition, non-psychoanalytic judges could also carry out blind analyses of the same case material.

Kedward (1969) found that the spontaneous remission rate showed little change in the period between a 1-year and a 3-year follow-up amongst 346 patients diagnosed by their general practitioner as having a psychiatric illness. The data are based on 82% of the original sample of 422 patients some of whom had only mild illnesses. At the 3-year follow-up, "73% of all new cases were regarded as free from psychiatric symptoms" (p. 3)—a similar proportion as those said to be recovered within a year. The study indicates that maximum remission occurs within a year and also that there is a minority of patients whose illness runs "a refractory course which continues longer than 3 years" (p. 3).

In their 5-year follow-up of 100 *neurotic* patients, Giel *et al.* (1964) found that 71% of the patients were recovered or much improved. In 90% of these improved cases the recovery had taken place within 2 years of their first attending an out-patient clinic. Although the rate of recovery observed in this group is consistent with the gross spontaneous remission rate, it cannot be quoted without reservation as one-half of the patients had received "at least a modicum of out-patient care and 20 patients were temporarily admitted to hospital". According to the authors, however, the untreated half of their sample did not show a different pattern of outcome to that of the treated group. "No difference was found between the outcome of these patients [i.e. treated] and the remainder of the group. Evidence was not available to show that their treatment had shortened their period of disability or relieved their subjective distress. This study therefore confirms that any new treatment for the neuroses must show better than 70% improvement before it can claim to represent a significant therapeutic advance" (p. 162). They were unable to find evidence of a relationship between outcome and a variety of variables including diagnostic category, degree of disturbance, sudden onset, and so on. However, 22 of the 24 cases with a history of less than 3 months' illness had a good outcome. In those 58 instances where they were able to date the patient's improvement, it was found to have occurred within the first year of the initial contact in 79% of the sample.

Although their attempts to obtain information about the prognostic variables involved in spontaneous remissions were unsuccessful, the small study reported by Endicott and Endicott (1963) is still of some interest. They carried out a 6-month follow-up of 40 untreated psychiatric patients, and although "the groups are too small to allow statistical analysis" it was found that 52% of the patients with neuroses or psychophysiological reactions improved, whereas only 9% of the "borderline" and schizophrenic patients were so evaluated. The authors themselves draw attention to some of the main limitations of their study. "From one point of view the most serious deficiency of the study was the brief duration of the waiting period" (p. 581). They add that "a second limitation is the small size of the patient sample, especially when the sample is divided into improved and unimproved groups" (p. 581). After the second evaluation, those patients who still wanted treatment were taken into psychotherapy, but "it is of interest that after the passage of 6 months only 12 out of the 33 remaining non-hospitalized patients still desired psychotherapy" (p. 537).

On similar lines, Cartwright and Vogel (1960) examined the characteristics of improvers and non-improvers—both before and during treatment. The study is difficult to evaluate as virtually no information about the patients is provided other than that "30 subjects who applied to the University of Chicago counselling centre for therapy were asked to participate in a research study" (p. 121). The patients' "pre-therapy status" and their changes with and without therapy were assessed on a Q adjustment scale and on the TAT. Unfortunately, 8 of the 30 subjects were lost before they had completed 6 interviews, and these "attrition cases" were excluded from the analysis. The remaining 22 subjects showed, on the whole, improvements during the pre-therapy period, and these improvements were apparently associated with longer waiting periods. Despite their ill-chosen outcome measures, the results obtained by the authors are worth mentioning. Even in the very short waiting period of 1–2 months, 5 out of 10 subjects reported positive changes on the TAT. Those 12 subjects who waited from 2 to 6 months before entering therapy showed evidence of greater change in that 6 of them reported positive changes on the Q-sort and almost all (9 out of 12) showed positive changes on the TAT. An evaluation of the effects of therapy is virtually precluded by the fact that the results on the two measures (the TAT and the Q-sort) tend to disagree. Incidentally, the claim by Cartwright and Vogel that self-report on the Q-sort "reflected their deep improvement on the conscious level in an improved self-description" is an odd remark. Presumably, advocates of the TAT would regard *their* findings as reflecting deep improvement as well.

In a more recent study, Jurjevich (1968) preferred to examine the spontaneous remission of particular symptoms rather than work in diagnostic categories. Two groups of 50 and of 62 psychiatric out-patients were re-tested on a symptom check-list after about 10 days or after 6 months. "Significant reduction of symptoms occurs after longer intervals [i.e. 6 months] on the raw and weighted full scales, raw scales of anxiety and psychosomatic complaints and weighted scales of anxiety immaturity and compulsiveness" (p. 199). Analysing the results in a slightly different way, the author found that 60% of the patients were improved within 6 months.

Jurjevich draws attention to the fact that "about one-third of the subjects do not seem to possess self-restorative mechanisms, tending to remain stable in their maladjustment or even to become worse. This finding gives support to the psychiatric rule of thumb that about two-thirds of patients recover with or without treatment and one-third remain unchanged in spite of treatment of various types if sufficient time is given for the operation of (spontaneous) homeostatic psychological processes" (p. 196). His analysis shows that of the 40% of patients who were not improved within 6 months, 13% were unimproved and 27% were worse. Detailed analysis of the symptom changes showed that the most changeable symptoms over the 6-month period included cardiac acceleration, twitching, bad dreams, and irritation. Although the overall findings are consistent with the gross spontaneous remission-rate estimate, the smallness of the sample and the relatively short period of observation place limitations on the generality of the data.

Cremerius (1969) has argued that there is a very small spontaneous remission rate in "organneurotischen Beschwerden". He selected from a polyclinic sample of 21,500 patients (seen between 1949 and 1951) those patients who had what can be described as "organ functional syndromes". This initial screening process produced no fewer than 7400 patients. A staggeringly high figure of this order (implying that every third patient attending the polyclinic had important neurotic features in his illness) raises serious questions about the nature of the diagnoses employed. An examination of the 6 groups of syndromes described by Cremerius feeds these doubts. The groups are: functional stomach syndromes; functional cardiovascular syndromes; functional syndrome of the lower digestive tract; functional respiratory syndrome; functional headache syndrome; functional ailments of a heterogenous and changing nature. In the functional respiratory group, for example, we find that patients with chronic bronchitis are included. It is possible that we are encountering linguistic problems because the terms *Neurosen* and *Psychoneurosen* are distinguished in German but rarely distinguished in English usage. For example, Psychrembel (1964) in his *Klinisches Wörterbuch* contrasts *Psychoneurosen* which are psychic disorders (and include behavioural disturbances and abnormal experiences) with *Neurosen* which are manifested in physical symptoms. It is extremely unlikely that Cremerius's large group of patients would be diagnosed as "neurotic" in a British or American polyclinic or general hospital.

Of the 7400 patients with organ neuroses, Cremerius selected 2330 (excluding those whose illnesses had lasted for less than 2 years) and sent them a letter requesting them to re-attend the clinic 11–30 years after initial admission. In other words, two-thirds of the sample were excluded and these exclusions ensured that patients with short-lived illnesses were not assessed. The remaining one-third of the sample who were contacted showed a very poor response. Only 15% (371 cases) re-attended as requested. Stated in another way, only one out of every potential 200 patients was reassessed. As noted above, patients with short-lived illnesses were specifically excluded. In addition, as will be shown presently, a comparable study carried out by Friess and Nelson (1942) indicated that the patients who failed to respond to this type of request for re-attendance show a disproportionately large number of recoveries. Moreover, it seems extremely unlikely that patients with distressing illnesses would fail to seek other treatment for 11–30 years after a diagnosis had been reached—and, indeed, there is internal evidence in Cremerius's paper to show that at least some of them were treated in the interim.

In view of all these limitations the Cremerius study can add little to our understanding of the spontaneous remission rate of neurotic disorders. For the record it is worth mentioning that the spontaneous remission rate was extremely low (8%) and the majority of patients either showed a persistence of the original difficulty or the original organ neurosis had changed to "psychic symptoms" (approximately 24%) or to physical syndromes (approximately 26%).

The views on spontaneous remission presented here have been challenged. Broadly, two types of criticism have been raised. It has been argued that neuroses do not remit spontaneously or, if they do, it is not a spontaneous process (e.g. Goldstein, 1960; Kiesler, 1966; Rosenzweig, 1954). Another point of view is illustrated by the work of Bergin (1970), who agrees that neuroses can remit spontaneously but that a more accurate estimate of the rate of occurrence of these remissions is in the region of 30%.

The claim that spontaneous remission of neuroses does not occur at all is a matter for demonstration rather than argument. The evidence described in this chapter, despite its shortcomings, seems to demonstrate its occurrence. The related but different question of whether or not "spontaneous remission" is an apt or a misleading description of the phenomenon can, of course, be debated. A satisfactory definition can be agreed upon, but even if such agreement is not obtained, the varying opinions on the subject are all capable of being defined in such a way as to prevent confusion. We can begin by dismissing those simple-minded views which suggest that the term spontaneous means "un-caused". It has been pointed out in previous publications that it is not the mere passage of time which produces an improvement in neurotic disorders; it must be events in time which are responsible (Eysenck and Rachman, 1965, p. 277). The attribution of causal influences is, of course, difficult, but it is wrong to give the impression that no theory exists which can come to grips with these questions. Eysenck (1963) has, in fact, proposed a theory of how and why spontaneous remissions occur and also of the circumstances in which spontaneous remission should not be expected to occur. It should be clear from earlier publications and the present work that the term spontaneous remission is used to describe improvements in neurotic disorders which occur in the absence of any formal psychiatric treatment. Undergoing a psychatric examina-tion (even with a possible view to later treatment) does not constitute treatment. Discussing one's problems with a relative, lawyer, priest, neighbour, or even a dark stranger does not constitute treatment. Events such as promotion, financial windfalls, and successful love affairs may all be therapeutic but, regrettably perhaps, they cannot be considered as forms of psychological treatment. These acts and events are all potentially therapeutic and undoubtedly contribute to the process of spontaneous remission. Current research interest in those events which precipitate psychiatric disorders encourages the hope that attention will also be turned to those events which have a *therapeutic* value. Within the context of an examination of the effects of psycho-therapy however, improvements in neurotic disorders which occur in the absence of formal psychological treatment can justifiably be regarded as "spontaneous".

On the question of quantitative estimates of the rate of spontaneous remission of neuroses, Bergin's (1970) estimate of 30% differs so widely from the present estimate that it is essential to examine his figures and arguments in some detail. Bergin begins by saying that "there has actually been a substantial amount of evidence lying around for years on this question". He concludes from this evidence that "generally, rates are lower than the Landis–Denker figures, thus justifying those critics who have emphasized the inadequacy or irrelevance of these baselines". Bergin then presents a table containing 14 studies, and he provides percentage improvement rates for each. As he remarks, the rates vary from 0 to 56% and "the median* rate appears to be in the vicinity of 30%!" Admitting that his figures "have their weaknesses", Bergin, nevertheless, feels that "they are the best available to date" and that they rest "upon a much more solid base than the Landis–Denker data". Before commencing a detailed examination of what Bergin considers to be the best available data, two points should be borne in mind. In the first place it seems to be a curious procedure in which one unearths new data and then calculates a median rate of improvement while ignoring the "old" data. The "new" data (actually some of them are chronologically older than those of Landis–Denker) should have been considered in conjunction with, or at least in the light of, the existing information. The second point is that although Bergin has considered some new evidence, he seems to have missed a number of more satisfactory and, indeed, more recent studies which are more pertinent to the question of spontaneous recovery rates. His estimate of a 30% spontaneous recovery rate is, in fact, based on 14 studies which are incorporated in table 8 of his work. It will be noticed immediately that the list omits some of the studies discussed earlier in this chapter.

The 14 studies are given with the percentage improvement rates quoted by Bergin. They are: Friess and Nelson (1942), 29%, 35%; Shore and Massimo (1966), 30%; Orgel (1958), 0%; Masterson (1967), 38%; Vorster (1966), 34%; Hastings (1958), 46%; Graham (1960), 37%; O'Connor et al. (1964), 0%; Cappon (1964), 0%; Endicott and Endicott (1963), 52%; Koegler and Brill (1967), 0%; Paul (1966), 18%; Kringlen (1965), 25%.

Bergin gives a spontaneous remission rate of 0% for Cappon (1964). The first surprise about Cappon's paper is its title—"Results of psychotherapy". He reports on a population consisting of 201 consecutive private patients "who underwent therapy between 1955 and 1960". Their diagnoses were as follows: psychoneurosis 56%, psychopathic personality 25%, psychosomatic reactions 8%, psychosis 8%, and others 3%. Only 10% received medication and 3.5% were hospitalized.

---

* In future studies, the inclusion of median rates *would* be helpful, particularly for prognostic use (Passingham, 1970).

As 163 had ended their therapy in 1960, "this was the operative sample". Cappon describes his treatment as being "applied Jungian". The results of the treatment were "admittedly modest", and the follow-up was conducted by mail. Unfortunately, only 53% of the patients returned their forms, and the follow-up period varied from 4 to 68 months. In addition, the follow-up sample "was biased in that these patients did twice as well at the end of therapy as rated by the therapist as those who did not return the forms". It is also noted that "the operative patient sample [$n = 158$] was still different [sicker] from a controlled normal sample, at the time of the follow-up. Patients showed more than 4 times the symptoms of normals. This ensured the fact that the sample was indeed composed of patients." The measure on which this conclusion is based is the Cornell Medical Index.

Cappon states that "the intention of this work was not so much to prove that results were actually due to psychotherapy as to show some of the relationships results. Consequently, there was no obsessive pre-occupation with 'controls' as the *sine qua non* dictate of science." We seem in the midst of all this to have strayed from the subject of spontaneous remissions. In fact, Cappon does make some brief comments on the subject. He argues that "if worsening rather than improvement were rated, 4 to 15 times as many patients changed [got worse] in the follow-up [control] period combined with the therapeutic [experimental] period, depending on the index used". He then argues that as the follow-up period averaged some 20 months and the therapeutic period some 6½ months, "this fact alone casts great doubt on Eysenck's data on spontaneous remission which led him to the false conclusion that patients did better without treatment than with treatment". Leaving aside the fact that Cappon unfortunately lost approximately half of his sample between termination of treatment and follow-up, we can perhaps leave uncontested his conclusion that many of the patients got worse after treatment. At best (?), Cappon's report adds support to the belief that some patients get worse after psychotherapy. It tells us nothing at all about spontaneous remission rates and, indeed, far from giving a spontaneous remission rate of 0%, Cappon does not provide *any figures* on which to calculate a rate of spontaneous remission. Bergin's figure of a 0% spontaneous remission rate would appear to be drawn from Cappon's introductory description of his patients in which he says that they "had their presenting or main problem or dysfunction for an *average of 15 years* before treatment" (original italics). Clearly, one cannot use this single-sentence description in attempting to trace the course of neurotic disorders or to determine their spontaneous remission rate. Nearly half of Cappon's patients apparently had disorders other than neurotic; we are not aware that they had been untreated prior to attending Cappon; we cannot assume that their diagnosis at the beginning of treatment would correspond with their condition in the years prior to treatment; we do not know whether the 201 patients constitute 90% of the relevant population or even 0.00001% of that population. Without labouring the point, we can disregard this incidental sentence as evidence for or against the occurrence of spontaneous remission and conclude that Bergin's use of these data is unjustified.

Bergin also gives a 0% spontaneous remission rate for the paper by O'Connor *et al.* (1964). Once again, the title—"The effects of psychotherapy on the course of ulcerative colitis"—is surprising as the subject under discussion is the spontaneous remission rate in neurotic disorders. Ulcerative colitis is defined by O'Connor and his co-authors as "a chronic non-specific disease characterized by inflammation and ulceration of the colon and accompanied by systemic manifestations" (p. 738). According to them, "its course is marked by remissions and exacerbations, its aetiology is considered multifactorial, and it has been variously attributed to infections, genetic, vascular, allergic, and psychological phenomena" (p. 738). It will not pass unnoticed that "psychological phenomena" are only 1 in a list of 5 types of attribution, nor, indeed, that the course of the disease is "marked by remissions". We have, then, some information of interest to gastroenterologists, namely that patients who have ulcerative colitis can show remissions. The study actually compares the progress made by 57 patients with colitis who received psychotherapy and 57 patients who received no such treatment. Apparently patients in both groups continued to receive medical and even surgical treatment. Nevertheless, as a group the ones who had psychotherapy did better overall. In the treated group, "19 patients were diagnosed as schizophrenic, 3 were psychoneurotic, 34 were diagnosed as having personality disorders, and 1 received no diagnosis". In the control group, however, "3 of the patients were diagnosed as schizophrenic, 3 as psychoneurotic, and 14 as having personality disorders. The remaining 37 control patients were not diagnosed because of the lack of overt psychiatric symptoms." As only 3 of the control group subjects were diagnosed as psychoneurotic, the spontaneous remission rate over the 15-year period would have to be expressed as the number of spontaneous remissions for a group with an n of 3. Bergin's use of the data in this report also raises a serious methodological point. He quotes the spontaneous remission rate for colitis patients as 0% over 15 years. In fact no such percentage rate can be obtained from the report as all the results are given as group means—in other words, it is perfectly possible and, indeed, likely that numbers of patients experienced remissions even though the *group* mean showed little change. For the study as a whole we are in no position to conclude what the spontaneous remission rate in 3 neurotic patients with ulcerative colitis was.

Orgel's (1958) report on 15 *treated* cases of peptic ulcer is quoted as showing a 0% remission rate. Bergin appears to argue that because the patients had suffered from stomach ulcers from 4 to 15 years prior to entering treatment, this indicates a remission rate of 0. Factually, Bergin is incorrect in stating that the peptic ulcers "had persisted from 4 to 15 years without change". Several of the patients had experienced remissions prior to entering psychoanalytic treatment. Furthermore, some of them experienced remissions and recurrences *during* the treatment. Far more serious, however, is Bergin's assumption that these 15 ulcer cases are representative of the relevant population—it is possible that 1500 cases not seen by the psychoanalyst experienced a different course in their illness. In addition, the introduction of material on the "natural history" of patients with *peptic ulcer* into a discussion on spontaneous remissions in neurotic disordeis is not justified.

In his table, Bergin quotes a 37% spontaneous improvement rate for a study by Graham (1960). In the text he says "Hastings (1958) found a 46% [spontaneous remission] rate for neurotics and Graham (1960) observed a range from 34 to 40% for sexual problems". What Graham actually reports in his brief paper is a comparison of the sexual behaviour of 65 married men and women before beginning psychoanalytic treatment with that of 142 married men and women who had been in treatment for from several weeks to 49 months. He found that for most (but not all) of the comparisons the patients in treatment expressed greater satisfaction in and greater frequency of sexual activity than did the patients awaiting treatment. Of course, this tells us nothing about the spontaneous remission of neurotic disorders. It is simply a comparison of the sexual activity of 2 groups of people at a particular point in time. We are given no details about the patients in either group—not their diagnosis, nor even their ages. We are told that before treatment the men in this sample ($n = 25$) showed a mean level of satisfaction of 2.81, but this figure is nowhere explained. We do not know what the range is, nor are we told how the figure is derived. At very best a study of this type might tell us what the spontaneous remission rate in sexual disorders is, but as we do not know what complaint these patients had or how they progressed, this study tells us nothing about the spontaneous remission rate in sexual (or neurotic) disorders.

From a study of the sexual life of potential patients, Bergin turns to a study which reports the fate of 10 juvenile delinquents (Shore and Massimo, 1966). As the patients comprising the untreated group of 10 were not suffering from neurotic disorders, their inclusion in an estimation of spontaneous remission in neuroses is difficult to justify. Although Bergin's discussion of this report adds nothing to our understanding of remission in neuroses, his handling of the data requires some comment. According to him, 3 of the 10 untreated delinquents remitted spontaneously (actually, on a basis of "known offences", the figure should be 4 out of 10). A major point, however, is that Bergin uses this figure of 3 out of 10 remitting to obtain a percentage remission rate of 30. This figure is then included in his table and added to other studies with much larger samples to yield a median rate of remission—surely a dubious way of proceeding. The point is emphasized by referring back to some of the studies which provided the material for a gross spontaneous remission rate. It will be recalled that the studies of Landis, Denker, and Shepherd and Gruenberg dealt with hundreds and even thousands of cases. In any event, readers interested in the "natural history" of delinquency may prefer to study the thorough and extensive investigation carried out by Teuber and Powers (1953).

We next turn to the Masterson (1967) study for which Bergin quotes a spontaneous recovery rate of "only 38%". Masterson reports the clinical status of 72 patients (from an original group of 101) who received treatment in an out-patient clinic during their adolescence. It is immediately apparent, therefore, that we are dealing not with an investigation of spontaneous remission but with a follow-up study of the effects of treatment administered during adolescence. We then learn that "during the 5-year follow-up period, 38 patients received out-patient treatment, 11 received in-patient treatment, and 31 received no treatment" (p. 1340). In other words, nearly 60% of the sample received further treatment during the follow-up period—hardly, then, a measure of spontaneous recovery. The matter is further complicated by the fact that Masterson used two methods for evaluating the psychiatric status of the patients. In the first place he apparently used the psychiatrist's "clinical judgement to rate the level of impairment of functioning". Later we read that "we re-defined impairment not in terms of functioning but in terms of underlying conflict with regards to dependency needs and sexual and aggressive impulses" (p. 1339). The level of impairment observed in 72 adolescents at follow-up is summarized by Masterson in a table on page 1340. A simple combination of the patients showing minimal or mild impairment at this stage yields a total of 27 out of 72—the source apparently of Bergin's conclusion that the sample showed a 38% spontaneous remission rate. It turns out, however, that relatively few of the 72 patients had a diagnosis of neurosis. In Masterson's own words, "breaking this down by diagnosis, we note that those with character neurosis did well, all having only minimal or mild impairment functioning, whereas those with schizophrenia and personality disorder did poorly, 75% having moderate or severe impairment of functioning. When the personality disorder group is further subdivided by type we find that 100% of the sociopaths, 63% of those with a passive aggressive disorder, 75% of the miscellaneous, and 8% of epileptics continued to have severe or moderate impairment of functioning" (p. 1340). If we now exclude the patients with schizophrenia and the psychopaths from our consideration, an interesting sum emerges. The remission rate, with schizophrenics and psychopaths omitted, is exactly 50%, but we hasten to add that this is *not* a spontaneous remission rate as an unspecified number of this remaining group received treatment during the period under consideration and also because some of the diagnostic labels (e.g. "passive—aggressive") are ambiguous. It can thus be seen that Bergin's statement that "Masterson found only 38% spontaneous recovery of adolescent disorders" is misleading.

Kringlen's study is described by Bergin as follows: "Kringlen (1965) followed the course of a sample of neurotics for 13 to 20 years and found that spontaneous changes varied with diagnosis. The overall spontaneous improvement rate was 25%." In fact the rate was neither spontaneous, nor was it 25%. Kringlen carried out a carefully conducted long-term follow-up study of 91 obsessional patients who were seen for 13–20 years after admission to hospital. On admission, "most of the patients got some form of somatic therapy, either ECT or drugs" (p. 714). Of these, 44% were improved on discharge. During the follow-up period "most of the patients received some form of treatment; 32 by drugs, 9 by ECT, 7 psychotherapy, 3 leucotomy, and 7 a mixture of several forms of therapy" (p. 716). Thirty-three of the 91 patients had received in-patient psychiatric treatment.

The outcome figures for Kringlen's patients, irrespective of type of treatment, were not too encouraging. Combining the cured, much-improved, and slightly improved groups, we find that only 28 (30%) had changed favourably at the *3-month* follow-up period, 46 (50%) at the *5-year* follow-up, and 44 (48%) at the 10-year follow-up period. We can only conclude from all of this that slightly under half of these obsessional patients were improved during a course of in-patient treatment and that the figure for the group as a whole increases only slightly after 5 or even 10 years—despite further treatment.

Bergin quotes Paul's (1966) experiment as yielding a spontaneous remission rate of 18%. He says that "after 2 years speech-anxious neurotic students spontaneously improved on speech anxiety at the rate of 22% and on more general anxiety at 18%". Bergin is perhaps justified in praising the thoroughness of this study, but unfortunately it tells us nothing about the spontaneous remission rate in neuroses and nor, indeed, was it designed to do so. It was concerned with the treatment of fear of public speaking. Contrary to Bergin's description, the students were *not* neurotic but were drawn from the normal undergraduate population of "710 students enrolled in public speaking" (Paul, 1966). Paul states that "students who, prior to contact, had entered treatment elsewhere or dropped the speech course were also excluded" (p. 25). He also points out that in the final screening of the subjects "those students who have received previous psychological treatment . . . were to have been dropped" (p. 25); in the event, however, "no subject needed to be excluded for these reasons". In other words, any student who had received psychological treatment, or was currently receiving such treatment, was automatically excluded. Moreover, each subject was subjected to extensive psychological investigation before and after treatment—no fewer than 5 types of psychological test were administered. The means obtained by the students on these tests did not fall into a neurotic classification on any of the 5 tests. A comparison between the mean scores obtained by Paul's "no-treatment" control subjects and those reported in an earlier study by Endler (1962) on a group of subjects drawn from the same university (Illinois) shows quite clearly the essential "normality" of the experimental subjects. The pre-treatment means for the control subjects are given first and are followed by the means recorded for the Illinois University undergraduates in 1962, which are given in parentheses. On the SR Inventory of Anxiousness sub-test entitled "contest", the mean was 33.4 (32.9); the "interview" item mean was 34.1 (31.62 with a standard deviation of 9.9); the "examination" item mean was 38.9 (37.6 and standard deviation of 10.9). On a measure of general anxiety, Cattell's IPAT, the mean was 35.6 with a standard deviation of 11.7 (34.5 and standard deviation of 7.4). For the Pittsburgh scales of extraversion and of emotionality, the normative data were reported by Bendig in 1962 on a sample of 200 students. Paul's subjects obtained a pre-treatment mean of 16.3 and Bendig's group had a mean of 17.6. On the emotionality scale, Paul's subjects had a mean of 17.8 with a standard deviation of 6.1 and Bendig's a mean of 14.6 with a standard deviation of 7.

The students used by Paul as experimental subjects in an analogue study cannot justifiably be included in an attempt to determine the spontaneous remission rate of neurotic disorders—any more than the large number of subjects who have been used in the numerous similar analogue studies (see review; Rachman, 1967).

Although the report by Hastings (1958) is not, strictly speaking, a paper on spontaneous remission rates, Bergin's inclusion of it is at least defensible. The spontaneous remission rate of 46% quoted by Bergin, while correct, needs some elaboration in order to be appreciated. Hastings followed up 1638 patients who were consecutive admissions to a psychiatric ward between 1938 and 1944. As the treatment available was extremely limited, he regards the outcome of these patients as a measure of spontaneous remission, and he also argues that it is most unlikely that these patients received further treatment during the follow-up period as they resided in a rural community. The follow-ups, which ranged from 6 to 12 years, were almost all conducted by interview (two-thirds of the original sample were interviewed). Among the neurotics, Hastings concluded that "taken as a group [371 cases] the outlook for satisfactory adjustment without specialized therapy appears fairly good" (p. 1065). Of this group, 46% were classified into the "excellent" or "good" outcome groups. However, it is probable that the outcome figures are deflated by the exceedingly poor outcome (25%) observed in the surprisingly large group who were diagnosed as suffering from "hypochondriasis"—no fewer than 95 out of the total of 371 cases. The 14 anxiety neurotics had a good outcome (65%), the 23 obsessionals moderate to poor (44%), and the 73 hysterics had a moderate outcome (56%). Although the figures obtained by Hastings do not reflect a true spontaneous remission rate—"minimal treatment rate" would be a better description—the findings are of some interest because of the personal assessments which were carried out and also because of the long follow-up period.

The study by Endicott and Endicott (1963) in which a 52% spontaneous remission rate was obtained over a period of 6 months is justifiably included in Bergin's table and has, of course, been discussed above.

Bergin's use of Vorster's (1966) paper is puzzling. He states that "Vorster (1966) reported that only 34% of his neurotic sample had improved after more than 3 years". Apart from some asides in the introduction, Vorster makes no mention of spontaneous remissions in his data. In fact he reports an 80% improvement rate in 65 treated neurotic patients, 55 of whom received private treatment. The age range of the sample was from 9 to 52 years and he provides meagre follow-up information. Twenty-four of the cases were followed up for either months or years. The results of the treatment were assessed by the therapist (i.e. Vorster himself). The treatment consisted of psychotherapy which varied from eclectic to "psychoanalysis bordering on the orthodox", narcoanalysis (beneficial in 7 out of 8 cases), some drugs, "temporary hospitalization", and "behaviour therapy" principles. An evaluation of Vorster's therapeutic claims is not our present concern. I have, however, been unable to trace the origin of the 34% spontaneous remission rate quoted by Bergin and willingly admit defeat.

Bergin's use of the report by Friess and Nelson (1942) is uncritical. He quotes two spontaneous remission figures: "Twenty of the no-therapy group of 70 had improved, or 35%." He then concludes that "thus, after 5 years and upon careful examination by skilled clinicians, these cases showed recovery rates less than half the rates reported among Landis and Denker's admittedly inadequate samples". The report by Friess and Nelson is a 5-year follow-up of patients who attended a general medical clinic in the period September 1932 to December 1933. The authors selected from the clinic records 498 patients from whom a *retrospective* diagnosis of psychoneurosis was determined. These 498 patients constituted 14% of the total clinic sample and 269 were traced in the follow-up study—i.e. just over half of the complete group. Of the 269 patients who were traced, 177 were interviewed, 69 were visited by a social worker, and/or supplied the information by post. The remaining patients were traced but little information was available as they were either in state psychiatric institutions or had died during the 5-year period.

The diagnoses seem somewhat atypical, and a substantial number of the patients can at most be regarded as suffering from psychosomatic disorders. For example, 111 (41%) had a diagnosis "referred to the gastrointestinal tract. In the order of their frequency the symptoms were abdominal pain, belching or flatulence, nausea, constipation, vomiting, halitosis, sore tongue, anorexia, difficulty in swallowing, and rectal pain" (p. 545). Fifty-seven of the patients had skeletal symptoms, mainly aches and pains in muscles or joints. Of the 269 patients only 7 had "phobias" (from the brief description supplied they were probably obsessional) and 4 of them had tics. As can be seen, this was scarcely a representative sample of neurotic disorders. No matter. If we examine the data on the *entire* sample of 269 patients we find that 115 had no psychiatric care whatever. This figure excludes the 15 patients for whom an incorrect diagnosis had been made and the 11 patients who had died during the 5-year period. We find that 50 of these untreated patients (i.e. 44%) were found to be either cured or improved. Sixty-five were found to be unchanged or worse (i.e. 55%). Of the total, 14 were categorized as "worse" and 1 was in a psychiatric hospital. Bergin's figure of 29% is an under-estimation of the spontaneous remission rate, but in this instance it can be explained. Before doing so, however, it is instructive to compare the spontaneous remission figures with the remissions found in the group of patients who had received "much psychiatric care". Of the 36 treated patients, none were cured and 10 got worse (including 4 in state psychiatric hospitals). Only 12 out of 36 showed any improvement. These figures can be compared with those reported for the patients who had received no psychiatric care. Of the 116 untreated patients in this group, 23 were cured, 27 were improved, and 15 were worse (including 1 in a state psychiatric hospital). Stated in a slightly different way, none of the *treated* patients was cured but one-fifth of the *untreated* patients were cured. If we combine the cured and improved categories, it is seen that 33% of the treated patients show some recovery, whereas slightly under half of the untreated patients were worse at follow-up, whereas only 8% of the untreated patients were found to be worse. Friess and Nelson sum up: "there was no noteworthy difference between the psychiatrically and non-psychiatrically treated groups" (p. 557).

Bergin's figure of a 29% spontaneous remission rate is obtained by relying exclusively on the patients who were interviewed at the end of the 5-year period, despite the fact that Friess and Nelson specifically draw attention to the higher remission rate obtained from those patients who did not re-attend the clinic when invited. They even mention 3 of the most prominent reasons given by the patients who declined the invitation. They were: there was no need to return to the clinic as they had improved; it was difficult or inconvenient for them to re-attend; they were dissatisfied with the treatment they had received. The essential point is, however, that the people who accepted the clinic invitation to re-attend were *demonstrably unrepresentative*. A significantly larger proportion of the refusers were well. Of the 48 untreated patients who refused the invitation to re-attend (but were later visited by the social worker and/or supplied information by post), no fewer than 30 were cured or improved. This yields a spontaneous remission index of 62% (10 patients were unchanged, 6 were worse, and 2 had been incorrectly diagnosed). If this finding were repeated in the 229 patients who were neither traced nor contacted (and this is a reasonable expectation), then the spontaneous remission rate would approximate the usual figure—despite the fact that it is doubtful whether the sample from this clinic is a typically neurotic one. If, however, we were unwise and decided to ignore the demonstrated distortion of the sample and we were also to suppress our doubts about the nature of the disorders under consideration, we would settle on the spontaneous remission rate of 44% described above. Fortunately, the shortage of adequate studies is not so desperate that it demands an unwise use of such doubtful information.

The study by Koegler and Brill (1967) does not provide figures on spontaneous remission rate, and is discussed in the section on psychotherapy (p. 78 below). In all, Bergin's substitution of a 30% spontaneous remission rate appears to be ill-founded.

In fact the available evidence does not permit a revision of Eysenck's (1952) estimate of a gross spontaneous remission rate of approximately 65% of neurotic disorders over a 2-year period. However, the evidence which has been presented since that original estimate was attempted emphasizes the need for more refined studies and more accurate statistics. In particular, it is now possible to say with a high degree of certainty that the gross spontaneous remission rate is not constant across different *types* of neurotic disorder. It is, for example, probable that obsessional disorders show a lower rate of spontaneous remission than anxiety conditions. Future investigators would be well advised to analyse the spontaneous remission rates of the various neuroses within rather than across diagnostic groupings. If we proceed in this manner it should eventually be possible to make more accurate estimates of the likelihood of spontaneous remission occurring in a particular type of disorder and, indeed, for a particular group of patients.

Although the gross spontaneous remission rate has thus far been based on a 2-year period of observation (and this serves well for many purposes), attempts to understand the nature of the process will, of course, be facilitated by an extension of the periods of observation. The collection of reliable observations on the course of spontaneous remission will, among other things, greatly assist in making prognoses.

Naturally, the determination of a reliable rate of spontaneous remission is only the first stage in a process of exploration. Both for its own sake and for practical reasons, we need to approach an understanding of the causes of spontaneous remission. Eysenck (1963) had adumbrated a theory to account for remissions and relapses which draws attention to the possible role of individual differences in personality. In addition, there are numerous bits of incidental information pertinent to the subject which are contained in clinical reports, follow-up studies, and the like (e.g. Stevenson, 1961). Respondents who have recovered from neurotic disorders often attribute their improvements to the occurrence of fortunate *events*. Some of the more commonly mentioned are financial gains, improvements in occupation, successful marriages and personal relationships, the amelioration of pressing difficulties, and so on (e.g. Friess and Nelson, 1942; Imber *et al.*, 1968). The identification of these restorative events and study of the manner in which they affect the process of remission would be of considerable value.

Unfortunately, the encouragement which can be derived from the occurrence of spontaneous remissions in neuroses must be tempered by recognition of the fact that a sizeable minority of patients do not remit spontaneously. Approximately one-third of all neurotic patients do not improve spontaneously, and it could be that in future it is this group of people who will absorb the attentions of clinicians and research workers. Such a redirection of effort must, of course, depend upon an accurate system of identification and prognosis. The size of the problem can be estimated from the current rates of rejection, defection, and failure reported by psychotherapists.

Recognition of the occurrence of spontaneous remissions in neurotic disorders leads us to consider the possibility (and utility) of establishing and determining an index of spontaneous deterioration. Although some neurotic behaviour (e.g. specific phobias) is unchanging, much neurotic behaviour is not stable, and it follows that the changes which occur can move in a positive or negative direction. Fortunately, the majority of the changes are towards improvement. It seems highly probable that a proportion of the remaining third who do not improve get *worse* over time. At present it is not possible to say much that is useful on this topic, but it is to be hoped that future studies of the course of neurotic behaviour patterns will also explore the occurrence of deteriorations and the factors which contribute to this process. In time it should be possible to determine the spontaneous remission index *and* the spontaneous deterioration index for various types of neurotic disorder.

CHAPTER 4

THE EFFECTS OF
PSYCHOANALYTIC TREATMENT

Two of the major conclusions reached by Eysenck in 1960 were: "when untreated neurotic control groups are compared with experimental groups of neurotic patients treated by means of psychotherapy, both groups recover to approximately the same extent", and "neurotic patients treated by psychoanalytic psychotherapy do not improve more quickly than patients treated by means of eclectic psychotherapy, and may improve less quickly when account is taken of the large proportion of patients breaking off treatment". These controversial conclusions have not been resolved to the satisfaction of all concerned, but there appears to be fairly wide (although by no means universal) agreement that the case for psychotherapy has not been proven. There is also general agreement on the need for controlled studies of the effects of psychotherapy and a recognition that reports of uncontrolled studies of psychotherapy are of little value. With the exception of psychoanalytic treatment, this book deals primarily with studies which have employed controls.

It was felt that psychoanalysis requires further examination even in the absence of controlled studies. Most forms of interpretive psychotherapy owe their genesis to a small or large extent to psychoanalytic theory and technique. Secondly, the evaluation of psychoanalytic results presents serious difficulties which are particular to it. Furthermore, even when a measure of agreement has been reached on evaluating other forms of psychotherapy, disputes about *psychoanalysis* continue. For example, Bergin (1970) is critical of many of the Eysenckian arguments and conclusions but finds himself in agreement with the conclusions regarding the effects of psychotherapy—other than psycho-analysis. He says: "while there are several modest differences between my and Eysenck's evaluation of the cases so reported, the overall conclusion is virtually identical. Eysenck finds a 64% improvement rate with a range from 41 to 77 and I find a 65% rate with a range from 42 to 87. I analysed 8 additional studies not reviewed by Eysenck and these yielded essentially the same mean and range of improvement." As Bergin observes, "it is striking that we should agree so closely on the results of eclectic psychotherapy and differ so sharply on our evaluations of psychoanalysis". For these 3 reasons it was felt to be necessary to include a discussion of psychoanalytic treatment even in the absence of suitable controlled studies.

An evaluation of psychoanalysis presents numerous difficulties, and one of the most serious is how to deal with the biases which operate in the selection of patients for treatment and the related problem of premature terminations of treatment. Recent information on these topics confirms earlier observations of a serious selection bias and a staggering-ly high rate of premature terminations—such that, even if one were to conclude that psychoanalysis is an extraordinarily effective treatment, it would be necessary to add the qualification that it has a remarkably narrow range of applicability. A second qualification would be that there is a strong risk that patients will not complete treatment. Again, even if one put the best possible face on the effects of psychoanalytic treatment, the premature termination rate demonstrates a serious deficiency in the criteria and techniques used by psychoanalysts in selecting patients for treatment.

One of the implications to flow from estimates of the gross spontane-ous remission rate in neurotic disorders is that any form of treatment for these disorders must attain a success rate as good as or, preferably, better than the gross rate. It is unlikely, however, that crude comparisons between treated and untreated groups of heterogeneous patients will advance our knowledge and understanding at anything more than a snail's pace. The more economic and sensible course is to attempt comparisons between treated and untreated groups of neurotic patients with similar disorders (and, hence, similar prognoses). On strictly scientific grounds the inclusion of untreated control groups is a pre-requisite for the evaluation of treatment techniques. The undesirability of withholding treatment from large numbers of patients (particularly where long-term follow-ups are envisaged) is too obvious to require elaboration. There are, however, several alternatives which can be employed such as "own-controls", brief waiting periods, placebo trials, and the rest (see the Strupp and Bergin 1969 review).

In any therapeutic evaluation study there are numerous problems to be contended with: diagnostic difficulties, outcome criteria, duration of treatment, patient selection and matching, and so on. Each of these problems becomes more prominent in attempting to assess the effects of psychoanalysis than is the case with other forms of treatment. Strict psychoanalytic theory implies its own somewhat idiosyncratic diagnostic concepts, criteria of success, the nature of failure, and, indeed, perhaps central to all of these, the *purpose* of treatment. Although frequently presented with outcome criteria such as "total functioning", which are as extravagant as they are nebulous, it is nevertheless possible to reach some agreed definitions (e.g. Knight, 1941). In my opinion, evaluations of psychoanalysis (and comparative studies) are difficult to contemplate until agreement is reached on the purpose of the treatment—i.e. are we trying to help the patient overcome his difficulties and complaints or are we hoping to change his "character structure" (see Hamburg, 1967)? It is not my present purpose to embark on an extensive investigation of these problems, nor do I wish to multiply or exaggerate the number and nature of these problems as they speak for themselves.

Most of the information on the effectiveness of psychoanalysis consists of single case reports (which we can largely discount in assessing effectiveness) and series of patients treated by a single analyst or, more commonly, at a particular clinic. We have, in addition, access to a few studies which have compared psychoanalytic and other types of treatment. Although some seemingly extravagant claims are made on behalf of the therapeutic value of psychoanalysis (e.g. "Psychoanalysis has emerged not only as the most effective method known for the study of the human psyche, but as the most effective method known for the treatment of emotional disorders" (Brody, 1962, p. 732), it is significant that the *authors* of the reports to be dealt with rarely make specific claims for the therapeutic value of psychoanalytic treatment. Indeed, in some instances specific disclaimers are recorded.

The most suitable starting point for an examination of the results of psychoanalytic therapy is the commendable survey attempted by Knight in 1941. He tried to remedy the fact that "to the knowledge of the writer there is not a single report in the literature on the therapeutic results of an analyst in private practice or of any such group of analysts" (p. 434). After carefully listing the great difficulties involved in his task, Knight proposed 5 criteria on which to base the outcome of treatment and then analysed the "brochure reports" of the Berlin Institute (1920–30), London Clinic (1926–36), Chicago Institute (1932–7), Menninger Clinic (1932–41), and the work of Hyman and Kessel. Each of these reports is analysed separately and jointly to provide a composite picture of the results. A total of 952 cases are listed by diagnosis and therapeutic result—with the appropriate words of caution on both scores. A specific point of importance is that the analyses of results from the Berlin, London, and Chicago clinics include only those patients who had completed *at least 6 months* of analysis. And, "in order to promote uniformity this same selection was used in the study of the Menninger Clinic cases and of course in the composite table . . . however, the writer is well aware that the excluded cases, i.e. those treated less than 6 months, represent an important group of 'failures' . . . it is emphasized here again that this group deserves special study, statistical analysis, and evaluation of the failure factors" (p. 438).

By its very nature the information compiled by Knight cannot provide us with an answer to the question of whether or not psycho-analysis is effective. Nevertheless, the interclinic and interdiagnostic comparisons are of some interest (especially for connoisseurs) and provide a general, if somewhat unclear, picture of analytic practice. Knight's overall conclusion, given in his composite table, is that the percentage cured and much improved rate for psychoanalytic treatment is 55.9%. Some additional information can be obtained by analysing sub-categories separately or in different combinations. For example, one can exclude the psychotic cases (who tended to do worse than neurotics) and the improvement-rate increases. On the other hand, if we include the 292 patients who broke off treatment before completing 6 months of analysis, then the overall improvement rate drops drastically. If we adopt both of these procedures (i.e. exclude the psychotics and include the premature terminators), we arrive at an overall recovery rate of 30%.

The interesting aspects of this information should not, however, cloud the main issue—these brochure reports do not demonstrate the effects—positive or negative—of psychoanalytic treatment.

Bergin (and others) have taken the view that premature terminations of psychoanalytic treatment should be excluded when one attempts to evaluate the efficacy of psychoanalytic treatment. As the majority of patients who break off the treatment appear to do so after having received what would be regarded by any other psychotherapist as a great deal of treatment, we are of the opinion that the terminators should be included as failures—unless there is demonstrable evidence to the contrary. There is, however, a more serious methodological problem lying beneath the surface. As will be shown presently, some accounts of psychoanalytical treatment claim astonishingly high rates of recovery (e.g. Bergin obtains a figure of 91%). It seems likely to us that these figures may be an artifact of the psychoanalytic procedure in that the therapist does not regard the patient as having completed his analytic treatment unless and until he has recovered. To take an extreme case, if a patient has failed to recover after 7 years of psychoanalytic treatment and consequently decides to discontinue attendance, then he would be regarded as a premature terminator rather than as a failed case. If one adopts the view, as most analysts do, that psychoanalytic treatment *is a complete treatment*, then it follows that failures can only occur as a result of an incomplete analysis. It is only by coming to grips with this viewpoint that one is enabled to understand why the premature termination rates are so high. Here we are forced to recall Galen's famous observation: "All who drink this remedy recover in a short time except those whom it does not help, who all die and have no relief from any other medicine. Therefore it is obvious that it fails only in incurable cases."* We might also note in passing that the average duration of psychoanalytic treatment is 3–4 years. As argued above, the spontaneous remission rate in neurotic disorders is approximately 66% over a

---

* See, for example, Brody's (1962) comments on the report of the American Psychoanalytic Association. He says that "one might draw the conclusion that of the patients who undertook analysis for neurotic reactions and completed treatment, 97% were cured or improved". Then, later on the same page (p. 732), he points out that "the patients who undertook analysis for neurotic reactions but did not complete their treatment, 50% discontinued because they were improved. The other half discontinued treatment because of external reasons."

2-year period—consequently one would expect a group of patients undergoing psychoanalysis to show an overall recovery rate in excess of 66%.

The questionnaire investigation of patients receiving psychoanalytic treatment, carried out by Bieber (1962), was procedurally similar to that conducted by the American Psychoanalytic Association (see below) but more successful. Seventy of the 100 members of the Society of Medical Psychoanalysts responded to a request that they complete questionnaires on homosexual male patients in their care. Every psychoanalyst was requested to complete 3 questionnaires, and in the event that they were treating fewer than 3 homosexuals they were asked to complete the questionnaires on heterosexual male patients. These heterosexual patients formed the comparison sample. The analysts were given "unrestricted choice" in the selection of comparison patients, and few of them had been in therapy for less than 100 hours. These initial questionnaires were supplemented later, and the sample of therapists was also extended. Varying degrees of information were finally obtained on 106 male homosexual patients and 100 heterosexual male comparison cases. As the authors point out, the samples were by no means random. In addition to the selection carried out by the responding therapists, the patient sample was unrepresentative of the general population, as in all the psychoanalytic reports and surveys emerging from the United States. The patients were predominantly from higher-than-average socio-economic classes, significantly well educated (two-thirds having completed university education), and two-thirds were in professional occupations. Obviously the selection bias and unrepresentative character of the samples preclude any generalizations about homosexual patients or their similarities and differences with other types of patient. The authors draw attention to these factors and mention, among other studies, the composition and nature of a British sample reported by Westwood (1960). The generality of Bieber's findings is further limited by the psychoanalytic bias incorporated in the questionnaires and interpretations placed on the data. Despite all these shortcomings, some interesting suggestions emerged from their extensive survey.

Of course, their comparison group is in no sense a control group and is irrelevant to a consideration of the effects of treatment. Their results cannot be used to prove or disprove the putative benefits of psycho-analytic treatment, but they are not without interest. Of the 106 homosexuals treated, 27% became exclusively heterosexual while 15 of the 30 patients who began treatment as bisexual eventually became heterosexual. Only 19% (14 out of 72) of those who began treatment as exclusively homosexual eventually became heterosexual. Only 7% of those patients who had fewer than 150 hours of treatment became hetero-sexual, whereas 47% of those who had 350 or more hours of analysis became heterosexual. The "favourable prognostic indicators" included bisexuality, motivation to become heterosexual, heterosexual genital contact at some time, under 35 years of age. The relevance of these indicators is discussed in Chapter 10.

In 1952 the American Psychoanalytic Association commendably set up a Central Fact-gathering Committee (Hamburg, 1967) in order to compile what is described as an "experience survey". All members of the Association were sent questionnaires to be completed on up to 25 patients per analyst. The Committee received approximately 10,000 completed questionnaires from about 800 participants (i.e. approxi-mately 80% of the analysts complied with this first request). The second questionnaire, entitled Final, yielded a far less satisfactory response, and they were able to obtain information on only 3000 patients. The initial report requested information on the vital statistics of patients and their presenting symptoms, while the final report requested informa-tion about the outcome of treatment. The loss of information on more than two-thirds of the patients is unfortunate, and the Committee was understandably puzzled by this sharp reduction in the number of participating analysts. They point out quite correctly that their sample is biased because of this lost material and "any conclusions based on this set of data must be qualified by our doubts about the representativeness of the sample" (p. 847). One need not take too seriously Brody's suggestion that the participating analysts failed to return the majority of the questionnaires because of "resistance" (Brody, 1962, p. 731). The important fact to bear in mind is that only 300 of the original 800 participants submitted final reports (i.e. outcomes) on neurotic patients who had been analysed. In addition it should be noted that the range of the number of patients reported per therapist was from 1 to 24, the mode being 1 patient report and the median about 6.

The Committee found that of the 595 cases of neurotic patients who had undertaken analysis, only 306 were reported as having been completely analysed, that is approximately 50%, and the average duration was 3–4 years. The Committee then sent follow-up questionnaires to the participants who had reported on the 306 completely analysed patients. They received only 210 replies, that is only 70%. Of these 210 supplementary questionnaires, 80 patients were listed as cured. In 35 of these, all of the symptoms were reported as cured and in 45 patients residual symptoms remained. In the 130 remaining questionnaires the improvement rates were high and the Committee concluded that "one might draw the conclusion that about 97% of the patients who undertake analysis for neurotic reactions and 'complete' it, are 'cured' or 'improved' ". Of the 50% who did not complete their analysis, about half discontinued apparently because they were improved. The other half discontinued because of "external" reasons or because they did not improve, or were considered untreatable, or they were transferred to other analysts, or required hospitalization. The most frequent reason given for discontinuing, apart from being improved, was "external reasons".

In the light of this striking improvement rate, some of the other findings of the Committee are a little surprising. For example, 650 analysts were asked about their expectations of treatment outcome, given a young person whom one could analyse for 4 years or more, with all conditions favourable. The analysts were asked to estimate the expected results for patients with neuroses, character disorders, and so on. The opinions were candid. Forty-five per cent of the analysts who replied "expected no cure in any of the conditions"!

Analysing the admittedly unrepresentative data, the Committee found that "96.6% of the patients reported that they felt benefited by their treatment". Similarly, 97.3% of the patients were "judged by their therapist to be improved in total functioning". Once more, "virtually all patients reported to their therapists that they felt benefited by completed treatment". Similarly impressive results were reported for the effect of treatment on the "character structure" of the patients.

There is only one finding which jars. The "overall incidence of symptom cure is only 27%". Whatever the temptation, these findings do not permit the provocative conclusion that psychoanalysis is capable of achieving everything except a removal of the patient's symptoms.

As already noted, the subgroup on which the data analysis was carried out is "significantly different from the parent group of 10,000 in the distribution of patients between psychoanalysis and psychotherapy, and in this respect, at the very least, is *not* a random sample" (p. 854). To this we may add the unknown effects which might arise from the *literal* loss of a great deal of the data between the inception of the study in 1952 and the appearance of the report some 15 years later. Moreover, an astonishingly large number of patients did not complete treatment. "Of the 2983 reports examined, 43% were in psychoanalysis, 47% in psychotherapy, and 10% in both at different times. Of those in psychoanalysis, 57% completed treatment and 43% did not. In psychotherapy these figures were 37% [completed] and 63% [did not]; in both, 47% completed and 53% did not complete." The Committee adds that "there is no information in the study as to whether termination was initiated by therapist or patient" (p. 854). The salient feature to emerge from all this is that *more patients terminated therapy prematurely than completed it.* The raw figures are as follows: 1589 did not complete treatment and 1393 did complete it. The Committee report contains little information about the patients who terminated their analysis before completion. It would appear from their inadequate figures that slightly under half of the premature terminators were "improved". Regrettably there are no data provided on the effect of an incomplete analysis on character structure, total functioning, or symptoms.

One of the more interesting aspects of this report and one for which the Committee can be commended is the information provided on the vital statistics of the patient sample. The Committee points out that the patient sample is highly selected and that they are grossly unrepresentative of the United States population. For example, 60% of all the patients were *at least* college graduates compared with 6% in the general population. The income and professional status of the group are both well above the United States average. In 94% of cases the treatment was carried out privately. The frequency of the treatment (in analysis) revealed that 61% of the patients attended their analyst 4 or 5 times per week. Approximately one-sixth of all the patients in this sample had undergone previous analyses. Nearly 7% of the sample were themselves psychiatrists (undergoing a training analysis).

The Committee expressed the view that the figures cannot "be used to prove analytic therapy to be effective or ineffective", and apart from providing some interesting peripheral information one hopes that this survey might prompt others to carry out scientific inquiries into the effectiveness of psychoanalytic therapy.

In 1961 Professor Barendregt of Amsterdam University published an interesting follow-up study of 3 groups of patients. These were derived from a number of patients who were tested psychologically when they applied for psychotherapy at the Institute for Psychoanalysis in Amsterdam. After about $2\frac{1}{2}$ years the patients were re-tested. Of these patients 47 (group A) had been given psychoanalysis; 79 patients (group B) had been given psychotherapy other than psychoanalysis, and not at the Institute; 74 patients (group C) did not have any form of psychotherapy or any therapeutic contact during the period. The follow-up study is concerned with a comparison of the changes which occurred, and it is obviously of central importance to know why patients were assigned to the various groups. It will be seen that this was not a control study in the ordinary sense but rather a comparison study which in its important respects should be thought of as retrospective. The "patients were classified into group B for various reasons. The decision in favour of psychotherapy for a number of patients was made for practical reasons (mainly financial), when psychoanalysis would actually have been more desirable . . . for some of the patients in group C psychoanalysis or psychotherapy was advised but impractical. Moreover, patients for whom psychoanalysis had been indicated and were put on a waiting list were included in the control group if by the time of the second psychological examination they were still awaiting treatment." Barendregt considers the possibility that selection may have vitiated the effects of any comparison between the groups but concludes that it is not too likely. The criteria of change were unfortunately not chosen with the care that might have been given, and included 2 projective tests of doubtful validity. A third reservation attaching to the study is the fact that the psychoanalytic treatment was carried out predominantly by inexperienced psychoanalysts.

The results of the study did not yield evidence in favour of the therapeutic usefulness of either psychoanalysis or psychotherapy. The positive outcome on one or two predictions relates to incidental effects; thus it is not the patient's sense of well-being or his neuroticism which is affected, but rather his score on the Lie scale, i.e. a score, the meaning of which is difficult to ascertain. The author concludes that "all the same this study is felt to have been useful. For one thing the patients' opinion of feeling better after some time of psychotherapy has proved to be of little meaning in favour of psychotherapy.* For another, the present study has shown 2 ways which may possibly lead to compelling evidence of the usefulness of psychotherapy. However, such evidence has not been arrived at by this investigation."

In their statistical appraisal of the putative effects of psychoanalytic psychotherapy, Duhrssen and Jorswieck (1969) compared the number of occasions on which 3 types of patient were admitted to hospital for any complaint in a 5-year pre-treatment period and a 5-year post-treatment period. The sheer number of hospital admissions was obtained from insurance cards, and the nature and cause of the admission was not specified in their study. Nonetheless, they compared 125 patients who completed psychoanalysis during 1958 with another 100 patients who were on a psychiatric waiting list and yet another 100 normal subjects. They found that there was no significant difference between the treated and untreated groups before psychoanalysis, but that both groups of patients had more admissions to hospital prior to treatment than did the normals. After psychoanalysis the treated group had fewer hospital admissions than had the untreated group, which showed no change in the number of days spent in hospital.

The authors' idea of using number of hospital admissions as an index of response to treatment is interesting but peripheral, and in the absence of direct evidence of the psychological state of the treated and untreated patients can tell us very little about the effects of psycho-analytic treatment. Their study also suffers from other defects such as a failure to explain why the treated patients *were* treated whereas the waiting list controls were not treated. One wonders why the untreated subjects were expected to or required to wait 5 years before receiving treatment—unless they did in fact receive treatment during the 5-year follow-up period. This point is not made clear in the paper. Certainly

* See also Koegler and Brill (1967, p. 55) for another example of this discrepancy.

one needs to know what type of patients they were and what sort of disorders they had that enabled them to wait patiently over a 5-year period while expecting to be given treatment. Another serious limitation of this study is the absence of *psychological* information about the patients and the curious but striking absence of any psychological assessment either before or after the treatment period.

Although Klein's (1960) paper is mainly concerned with the putative changes which occur during psychoanalytic treatment, some of the information is relevant to the present discussion. She carried out a retrospective analysis of 30 patients who had completed a minimum of 200 analytic sessions (4–5 times weekly), who had been out of treatment for more than a year and who had an original diagnosis of neurosis. The "arbitrary length of treatment" chosen in this study "automatically rules out those patients whose psychoanalytic treatment at the clinic is discontinued early" (p. 156). Klein admits that "this procedure may appear to favour a trend of excluding treatment failures . . . but we were interested primarily in finding a method for studying therapeutic changes" (p. 156). The degree of selection involved in assembling these 30 patients is indicated by the fact that they were chosen from an original group of 288. The demographic characteristics of the 30 patients are comparable to those reported by the Fact-finding Committee of the American Psychoanalytic Association (p. 50). Klein's description of the criteria for selecting patients for psychoanalytic treatment at the clinic (Columbia University Psychoanalytic Clinic) is of interest. The patient "must possess sufficient motivation to improve his current functioning". The assessing psychoanalyst then attempts to assess the patient's degree of rigidity and his ego strength. In both instances they have to be favourable before the patient is considered suitable for treatment. In addition the patients whose "prognosis is most favourable and who are, therefore, regarded as most suitable for psychoanalytic treatment are those who present structured symptomatology of a relatively short duration" (p. 155). Furthermore, the selected patients "are expected to be capable of a degree of effective functioning, either currently or in the recent past". Again, "these patients must be capable of significant pleasure response". To complete the list, the patients must "have the ability to form affective relationships with others and a history of having been capable of such relationships with others in the past". It is reassuring to learn that "these basic criteria of psychoanalysability are used flexibly" (p. 155).

The selection of patients for this retrospective study was based on the diagnosis made at the end of the third month of treatment, and patients with "schizotypal disorders" were excluded as it is the policy of the clinic not to undertake treatment of these patients by standard psychoanalytic technique. In view of the formidable list of excluding criteria and the apparent intensiveness of the screening procedures, it comes as something of a surprise when we are told that at the time of the follow-up study "7 of the 30 cases, originally diagnosed as psychoneurosis, were diagnosed schizotypal disorder by the 5 interviewers" (p. 170).

It was found that 76% of this group of 30 patients rated themselves as having shown considerable improvement at the follow-up period.

This favourable outcome was consistent with the conclusion reached by the psychoanalytic raters who examined the case notes of each patient. It is, however, necessary to qualify the impression given by these overall results. The ratings made by the psychoanalytic judges were not blind. The raters were aware that the patients had completed analytic treatment and also "had the knowledge of the patients' functioning at all 3 periods when rating any one period". Secondly, "about one-half of the patients in our sample" had had previous therapy. There would appear to be a strong likelihood that the sample under consideration is far from being representative, and the absence of any control group is, of course, an obvious shortcoming. Finally, it is noted that after the follow-up "more than one-fourth of the group had returned to treatment with an analyst, usually on a 1–2 times per week basis" (p. 165).

The serious problem of selection bias in any attempts to assess the effects of psychoanalysis is underscored by some incidental information which emerges from the work by Knapp and others (1960) who attempted to determine criteria for successful analytic treatment. Like Klein and the Fact-gathering Committee, these workers found that analytic patients had a disproportionate number of highly educated and sophisticated patients. For example, in their sample of 100 cases no fewer than 64 had received postgraduate education. Seventy-two per cent were in professional and academic work and approximately half of all the cases were "engaged in work related to psychiatry and psychoanalysis" (p. 463). They also found that "interviewers accepted approximately one-third of all applicants". The wholly unrepresentative nature of the patients who receive psychoanalysis (at least in the United States) is confirmed by the work of Hollingshead and Redlich (1958).

The marked bias operating in the selection of patients who are chosen for psychoanalytic treatment would, of itself, make any attempts at generalization about the effects of the treatment risky. As noted above, the extremely high rejection rate is further compounded by the unacceptably large number of patients (roughly one-half) who terminate treatment prematurely. Rightly or wrongly, psychoanalysts appear to believe that their method of treatment is suitable only for a tiny fraction of the population of psychological cases in the community. Moreover, in considerations of social utility, one has to bear in mind that psychoanalysis is extremely time-consuming. Given that the average course of analytic treatment takes 3–4 years,* and that an analyst using classical analysis is unlikely to carry more than 8 patients at any one time, we estimate that a practising psychoanalyst will complete treatment on roughly 2 or 3 patients *per year*. Carrying these calculations a little further, we find that a psychiatric clinic or hospital which aims to complete treatment on a thousand cases a year would require in the region of 300–500 full-time psychoanalysts.† Viewed in this perspective it seems reasonable that if psychoanalytic treatment is to be practised, then we have grounds for expecting it to do more than provide relief for a highly selected and tiny group of people (e.g. it could be argued that the treatment process might increase our understanding of psychological processes or mechanisms). The point is that judged on grounds of social utility, psychoanalytic treatment has little justification. Naturally, its scientific value needs to be judged by other criteria (e.g. Wolpe and Rachman, 1960; Rachman, 1963). The scientific, medical, and social aspirations were severely dealt with in a recent examination conducted by a doyen of British psychiatry (Slater, 1970).

The comparative study reported by Cremerius (1962) is unfortunately defective in the same respect as the Barendregt study in that the selection

---

* United States Committee's figures. At the London Psychoanalytic Clinic, the average duration of treatment is given as 41 months (*Rep. Br. Psa. Society*, 1967).

† In 1967 the entire British membership of the Psychoanalytic Society was 300 and, of course, this includes non-practising members.

of patients for psychoanalytic treatment was not random. In both studies there was a very careful selection of patients, and those thought most likely to benefit from psychoanalytic treatment were given prime choice and constituted a small minority of the total patient pool. As we have already seen in earlier reports, those patients who are selected for psychoanalysis are a highly unrepresentative sample of the population and include a grossly disproportionate number of highly educated, persistent patients from the middle classes. The Cremerius report deals with the fate of 605 neurotic out-patients who were treated by some form of psychotherapy during the period from 1948 to 1951. A further 175 patients were excluded because they were not considered suitable for psychotherapy either because they refused treatment, were of an inappropriate age, or where suspected of having a psychotic disorder, etc. The majority of patients were between 30 and 50 years of age and the sexes were equally distributed. About one-third of the patients expressed a wish for psychotherapy and about one-half had no idea of what psychotherapy was and had no desire for such treatment. These ideas and views played a considerable part in the selection of therapy. Nine per cent (56 cases) were treated by analytic therapy, 160 cases (27%) by verbal discussion and psychotherapy, 194 (32%) received hypnotic treatment, 40 cases (7%) had narcohypnotic treatment, 105 (17%) received autogenic training, and 50 cases (8%) received a combination of treatments. A majority of patients who were psychoanalysed had psychosomatic symptoms, whereas very few of those who received hypnosis or narcohypnosis had such a diagnosis. The treatment allocations correlated highly with social class in the expected direction.

The figures for the outcome of therapy in 573 cases are shown in Table 1. The criteria for outcome of treatment were the same for all groups, but it will be noticed that the outcome categories given at the end of treatment do not include patients who were unchanged or worse at the end of treatment. For the total sample, the overall improvement rate is 78%. The figures at termination of treatment are most favourable for hypnosis and least favourable for combined treatment methods. Psychoanalysis is inferior to hypnosis and superior to the combined method and seems roughly comparable to autogenic training as far as success rate at termination is concerned. The proportion of patients who abandoned therapy (presumably this figure includes unchanged or

TABLE 1

THE EFFECTS OF DIFFERENT TYPES OF THERAPY (Eysenck's 1969 account of the Cremerius study of 1962)

Therapy	Position at end of treatment			Position at follow-up		
	Abolition of symptom (%)	Symptom improve-ment (%)	Treatment terminated (%)	Abolition of symptom (%)	Symptom improve-ment (%)	Symptom substitution or worsening (%)
Analytic psycho-therapy	41	29	30	21	31	18
Verbal discussion	48	33	19	12	13	37
Hypnosis	54	31	15	7	10	47
Autogenic training	38	32	30	12	17	28
Combined methods	32	26	42	7	14	39
Total	47	31	22	11	14	37

deteriorated cases as well) was largest for psychoanalysis and autogenic training. This failure (?) rate occurs in spite of the rigorous selection which isolated those patients deemed most likely to succeed with psychoanalytic treatment. Within diagnostic categories, hysteria and anxiety neuroses showed the best results with the remarkable figures of 97% and 94% of "cures and improvements". Depression, hypochondria, and obsessional disorders did rather less well and showed fewer instances in which the symptoms disappeared. However, 92% of all patients were at work at the end of treatment compared with only 63% prior to treatment.

The follow-ups were carried out between 8 and 10 years after termination and the excellent figure of 86% were traced. The figures are shown in Table 1, but those cases in which the symptom remained unchanged (38%) have been omitted. One of the most unstable features of the follow-up figures is the sharp reduction in the overall percentage of improvements—a fall from 78% to 25%. The most striking change is the large deterioration in the group of patients treated by hypnosis. The patients who received psychoanalytic treatment show a much smaller deterioration and the difference between these two types of treatment at follow-up is statistically significant. In addition to this difference between treatment types, the figures also suggest some differences in outcome for diagnostic categories. These figures are shown in Table 2.

TABLE 2

THE EFFECTS OF THERAPY ON DIFFERENT DIAGNOSTIC GROUPS (Eysenck's account of the Cremerius study of 1962)

	Condition at follow-up				
	Symptom abolition (%)	Symptom improvement (%)	Symptom unchanged (%)	Symptom worse (%)	Symptom substitution (%)
Hysteria	9	11	24	3	53
Anxiety state	9	12	31	3	45
Obsessive–compulsive	5	10	67	9	9
Hypochondria	6	13	52	21	8
Neurasthenia	8	16	29	5	42
Neurotic depression	12	15	19	14	40

They indicate a marked degree of so-called symptom substitution, and this is particularly noticeable in hysterics but appears also in anxiety conditions and depressions. The hypochondriacal group shows a large number of patients who got worse and the obsessionals an extremely high percentage of patients with unchanged symptomatology. Two-thirds of the patients with this disorder show little variation in their condition over an 8- to 10-year period. As mentioned earlier, the most striking feature of these figures is the exceedingly poor recovery rate over the long term—averaging only 25% compared with the figure of 73% improved at termination of therapy. The suggestion that patients who received psychoanalytic therapy do slightly better over the long term despite the absence of any such superiority at the time of treatment termination is interesting and might be worth investigating in a more appropriate control study where the selection of patients is correctly randomized. It should be noted that those patients who received psychoanalytic treatment had far more treatment than had the patients in other groups. They received in the region of approximately 300 hours of treatment as opposed to a dozen hours or less for some of the other groups. Another important comparison would, of course, involve types of treatment more frequently used in Britain and the United States. In terms of Anglo-Saxon practice, the German methods are unusual.

The study reported by Phillips (1957) also compares an unorthodox method with psychoanalytic treatment. The comparison treatment was developed by Phillips and is based on "interference" theory. Very briefly, interference theory states that behaviour is a result of various assertions made by the individual about himself or about his relationship with others. The person chooses one kind of behaviour, now another, depending on what kind of behaviour seems likely to bring (from the environment) confirmation of his assertions. Certain behaviour possibilities "interfere" with each other, i.e. the person cannot do both at the same time. However, since possible behaviour is always selected by a person on the basis of its appropriateness to the environment, the whole process with which we are concerned goes on "in the open". "Depth views which regard the mental life of people as having a kind of reservoir from which diabolical forces spring are entirely anathema to the present viewpoint" (Phillips, 1957).

The treatment used by Phillips is directive and involves an analysis of his patient's prevailing difficulties and choices. The problems are examined with the guidance of the therapist and the most desirable practical possibilities are then encouraged in a form of behavioural prescriptions.

Before comparing the effects of this treatment with that of analysis, it should be noted that the samples of the 2 groups were selected on quite different principles, and for this reason (among others) the study cannot be regarded as a satisfactory test of either treatment technique. The results of the comparison are shown in Table 3. Before turning to the table, however, it should be noted that the number of interviews required by the interference method was less than half that required by psychoanalytic methods, a difference which was statistically significant. On the basis of his research, Phillips argues that the results "suggest strongly that there are real differences in the effectiveness and efficiency of out-patient, parent–child psychotherapy when assertion therapy and

TABLE 3

A COMPARISON BETWEEN DEPTH THERAPY: PHILLIPS'S THERAPY AND A HYPOTHETICAL IDEAL. Quoted from E. L. Phillips (1957), *Psychotherapy: A Modern Theory and Practice*, Staples, London

	1 Number applying for therapy	2 Number treated from among applicants	3 Number refused treatment by clinicians	4 Number who themselves refuse treatment	5 Number completing 3 or more interviews	6 Number benefited by 3 or more interviews	7 Percentage of original applicants benefited
Hypothetical group	100	90	5	5	90	90	81
Assertion-structured therapy	59	53	—	6	53	51	86.4
Psychoanalytic depth-oriented therapy	190	45	103	42	45	21[a] (patients' rating) 33[a] (therapists' rating)	11.05[a] (patients' rating) 17.3[a] (therapists' rating)

[a] Therapists' ratings were available for all 45 patients who completed 3 or more interviews. Only 27 of these 45 patients returned questionnaires rating their therapy experience; the 21 who rated themselves as having improved somewhat supplied the figure used here.

psychoanalytic-derived depth methods are compared". Particularly striking in looking at the figures for psychoanalytic therapy is the fact that of all those applying for therapy only 25% (45 out of 190) were actually accepted for therapy. Apart from the wider import of these high rejection figures, their occurrence creates enormous difficulties for anyone attempting to assess the affectiveness of psychoanalytic treatment. The outcome figures show that 51 of the 53 children were benefited by Phillips's therapy but only 21 out of 45 were so benefited by psychoanalytic therapy—a significant difference.

Phillips concludes very firmly that "one may produce certain arguments against interpreting these results as being in any way adverse as far as psychoanalytic depth-derived, parent–child, out-patient treatment cases are concerned. One might say that the methods used are not 'true psychoanalysis' of children. However, the record of 'true' psychoanalysis of children is hardly better, if as good: witness the work of Klein and Anna Freud. The argument for depth-derived practices cannot be bolstered on the basis of probable value latent upon unstudied and unreported upon therapeutic results . . . the hard reality here is that there are not convincing results of a follow-up nature that can be used to support psychoanalytically derived treatment of children."

A fourth study comparing psychoanalytic and other types of psychotherapy was reported by Ellis (1957). Ellis has himself used psychoanalytic psychotherapy of the orthodox type in addition to psychoanalytic-type psychotherapy and also what he calls "rational psychotherapy". Briefly, "the main emphasis of the therapist . . . is on analysing the client's current problems . . . and concretely showing him that these emotions arise, not from past events or external situations, but from his present irrational attitudes toward, or illogical fears about, these events and situations". Two groups, closely matched as to diagnosis, age, sex, and education, were constituted. Each consisted of 78 cases and the first group consisted of patients treated with rational techniques over an average period of 26 sessions. The second group of 78 patients was treated with psychoanalytic oriented techniques over an average of 35 sessions. In addition there was a group of 16 patients who were treated by orthodox psychoanalysis over an average of 93 sessions. They were all treated by Ellis himself and he rated them at the termination of treatment in terms of whether the patient had made (a) little or no progress while being seen, (b) some distinct improvement, or (c) considerable improvement.

Ellis found that "therapeutic results appear to be best for patients treated with rational analysis and poorest for those treated with orthodox analysis . . . significantly more clients treated with rational analysis showed considerable improvement and significantly fewer showed little or no improvement than clients treated with the other two techniques". The actual proportions of cases showing distinct or considerable improvement were 90% for rational psychotherapy, 63% for psychotherapy, and 50% for orthodox psychoanalysis. These figures should be seen in the light of the fact that orthodox analysis was carried on for 3 times as many sessions as rational psychotherapy. Ellis concludes that "while the obtained data of the study do not offer incontrovertible proof of the superiority technique of rational psychotherapy, they strongly indicate that neither orthodox nor liberally psychoanalytical procedures may be the very last word in effective technique".

Of course, without the use of an appropriate control group it is impossible to say whether the patients treated by rational psychotherapy did better than those treated analytically because rational therapy had a positive effect or because analytic therapy had a negative effect. The former appears to be the more likely hypothesis but cannot be confirmed or disconfirmed in this study (rater contamination, poor outcome criteria, etc.).

With the exception of the study by Barendregt, all of these comparison studies involve psychoanalysis matched against some form of treatment about which little is known with certainty. This fact, coupled with the other limitations involved in all of the studies (including Barendregt's), do not allow a definite conclusion. In none of the studies was psychoanalysis shown to be superior at the termination of treatment; in 2 studies it was found to be worse and in 1 study it was found to be equally effective at termination and superior over the long term. Clearly what is needed is a sound comparative study and, if possible, the inclusion of an untreated control group. Because of the obvious difficulties involved in any long-term study of untreated patients, perhaps the best we can hope for at the moment is a carefully controlled comparison study between psychoanalysis and one of the more widely used treatment techniques, e.g. conventional supportive psychiatric care and/or drug treatments, and—most interesting of all perhaps—behaviour therapy.

There is still no acceptable evidence to support the view that psychoanalytic treatment is effective.

CHAPTER 5

THE EFFECTS OF PSYCHOTHERAPY

WITH few exceptions, psychologists appear to have accepted the need for satisfactory evidence to support the claim that psychotherapy is beneficial. Most writers also appear to accept the view that in the absence of suitable control groups, investigations cannot provide a conclusive result. Working within these terms of reference, several writers (Cross, 1964; Dittmann, 1966; Kellner, 1967; Bergin, 1970) have concerned themselves primarily with the evidence emerging from studies incorporating control groups. In most instances it is concluded that there is now modest evidence to support the claim that psychotherapy produces satisfactory results. It is, however, a little dispiriting to find that with successive reports, the claims appear to become increasingly modest.

Although there is a continuing theme in these discussions on the outcome of psychotherapy, the writers concerned are by no means in agreement. Discussing the earlier reviews, Bergin says "Cross (1964), for example, reviewed 9 control studies and determined that 6 were favourable to therapy, whereas our own review of the same reports yielded only 1 that approximated adequacy and even that one is subject to criticism (Rogers and Dymond, 1954). Dittmann (1966) added 5 more studies to Cross's group, considered 4 of them to be positive evidence, and concluded that 10 out of 14 controlled outcome studies were favourable to psychotherapy. Actually, only 2 of the studies indicate that psychotherapy had any effect and neither of them would be generally acceptable as evidence. Thus, these authors claim *strong* support for the average cross-section of therapy, whereas I would argue for a more modest conclusion." While I agree with Bergin's assessment of these reviews, it should in fairness be pointed out that both Cross and Dittmann were more tentative and cautious than Bergin allows. For example, Cross mentions that some important "cautions must be kept in mind". The work referred to in his review consisted of "quite brief or superficial" treatment, the measurement techniques were "of questionable or unproven validity", and for some of the studies "the method of control itself is questionable". For these reasons he specifically urges caution: "even though the reviewed studies are the most careful which have been done, various limitations prescribe any strong conclusions" (p. 416). It should also be remembered that 4 of the largest and best-designed studies produced *negative* results—Teuber and Powers (1953); Barron and Leary (1955); Fairweather and Simon (1963); Imber *et al.* (1957). In regard to the last-mentioned study, Cross placed a more optimistic interpretation on the data than did the authors themselves. As will be shown below, the authors made no claims for psychotherapy, and their findings were sometimes contradictory, often fluctuating and, finally, inconclusive. Cross himself points out that the Rogers and Dymond study uses a questionable method of control, and this investigation is also discussed below.

Bergin's rejection of the conclusion reached by Dittmann is understandable. Even Dittmann, however, has his reservations: "My impression is that studies of the outcome of psychotherapy have finally allowed us to draw conclusions on other bases than intuition, but the conclusions, themselves, are modest, and are, moreover, diluted by confusion." All the same, he felt that 1966 was "a year of bumper crop in outcome studies". Dittmann claims that 4 out of the 5 control studies described by him were favourable to the position that psychotherapy is effective. Two of these studies can be dismissed immediately. The first is the study by O'Connor *et al.* (1964) referred to in an earlier section (p. 31). It deals with 57 patients with colitis who also received psychiatric treatment. Their 57 so-called control subjects, like the treated ones, received medical and even surgical treatment during the course of the study. Moreover, the treated patients were said to have psychiatric problems while only a minority of the controls were so described. A second study quoted by Dittmann used as the criterion for improvement after psychotherapy a measurement of "time perspective" as interpreted on the basis of TAT stories (Ricks *et al.*, 1964). The study by Seeman and Edwards (1954) involved very small numbers of children and, in any event, on one of the major outcome criteria (teacher ratings) no differences emerged. The report by May and Tuma (1965) showed that patients given drugs improved more than those who did not receive drugs; it produced no evidence that psychotherapy was effective. The study by Ashcraft and Fitts (1964) cannot be assessed satisfactorily because they used an unpublished test as their criterion of outcome. As Dittmann allows, "the results are complicated because of the many subscores of the test and the methods of analysis, but clearly favour the treatment group".

As measurements of the self-concept feature prominently in outcome studies and the notion of changes in self-concept is also a central feature of non-directive therapy, it seems desirable to examine the idea and its measurement in detail. Such an examination may also be thought of as being instructive in so far as the assessment of assessment is concerned.

Self-concepts

Wylie (1961) has neatly summarized the predictions which flow from theories of self-concept psychotherapy. It is to be expected that successful therapy will produce various changes in self-concept, such as the following: "increased agreement between self-estimates and objective estimates of the self . . . increased congruence between self and ideal-self, if this congruence is very low at the outset of therapy . . . slightly decreased self-ideal congruence if this congruence is unwarrantedly high at the outset of therapy . . . increased consistency among various aspects of the self-concept" (p. 161).

Wylie mentions, among other difficulties, many of the problems involved in attempts to relate changes in self-concept to psychotherapy. Two of the major problems are the possibility of mutual contamination between measures of improvement and measures of self-concept (p. 165) and the serious problems of scaling. (For example, "neither can one say that equal numerical changes involving different scale ranges are psychologically comparable" (p. 166).) Like Wylie, Crowne and Stephens (1961) draw attention to the large variety of tests which have been evolved to measure self-regard, self-acceptance, and the like. They comment unfavourably on the assumption that these tests are equivalent "despite their independent derivation and despite the relative lack of empirical demonstration that there is a high degree of common variance among them" (p. 107). They point out that there is a serious absence of information on both the reliability and validity of these tests. For example, "criterion validation of self-acceptance tests is, of course, logically impossible . . . face validity, however, has apparently been assumed without question (and this) implies adherence to a further assumption . . . that of the validity of self-reports. In terms of these assumptions, a self-acceptance test is valid if it looks like a self-acceptance test and is similar to other tests and what a person says about himself self-evaluatively is accepted as a valid indication of how he 'really' feels about himself" (p. 106). Another major difficulty with these tests is the often dubious assumption that the items chosen represent a fair sample of the possible parameters. They argue that it is "of importance to draw one's sample of test items in such a way as represent their occurrence in the population". Although they are not entirely consistent on this subject, writers generally assume that the self-reports given by subjects are valid. Crowne and Stephens draw attention to reports of extremely high correlations between self-concept rating scales and social desirability scales. In one study, for example, the correlations between Q-sort and a social desirability score were found to be 0.82, 0.81 and 0.66. Social desirability correlated 0.82 with the ideal-self rating scale score and 0.59 with the ideal-self Q-sort. In a study conducted on students, correlations of 0.84 and 0.87 were found between items on a Q-sort and a social desirability scale. In a psychiatric sample the correlation was found to be 0.67. Another study quoted by them produced what is probably a record correlation of 0.96 (between social desirability and an ideal-self score). They conclude quite firmly that "failure to control for social desirability in the self-acceptance assessment operations would make the results, no matter what the outcome, uninterpretable in terms of self-acceptance" (p. 116). They even go so far as to suggest that in the absence of suitable controls, the tests in question "may better be interpreted as a measure of social desirability than of self-acceptance".

In all, Crowne and Stephens were unimpressed. "The failures of self-acceptance research can be traced, at least in a large part, to neglect of several crucial psychometric and methodological principles: the unsupported assumption of equivalence of assessment procedures, the absence of any clear construct level definition of the variable, failure to construct tests in accord with principles of representative sampling, and questions concerning the social desirability factor in self-report tests" (p. 119). Although not as harsh in their judgements, Lowe (1961) and Wittenborn (1961) are also critical of self-concept procedures.

Moving from a consideration of the general status of self-concept research, we may now examine its specific application in the assessment of abnormal behaviour and the effect of psychotherapy. We strike an immediate difficulty in attempting to define the relationship between the self-concept and adjustment. Although there is fairly good agreement that low self-regard is related to maladjustment, high self-regard may indicate one of *three* things. It may be a sign of good adjustment or of denial of problems or, yet again, of "unsophisticated conventionality" (Wylie, 1961). For example, Crowne and Stephens mention a study by Bills in which subjects with high self-acceptance scores were found to be more maladjusted than low scorers. Summarizing a good deal of the literature, Wylie concluded that "there is much overlap between groups" (i.e. neurotics, non-psychiatric patients, normals). Comparisons between psychotics and normals have been contradictory with at least "3 investigators reporting no significant difference between psychotic and normal controls" (p. 216). Considering the range from normal through various types of abnormality, she concludes that "a clear linear downward trend in self-regard is *not* found" (p. 216). In 4 studies, in fact, a curvilinear relationship between self-regard and severity of maladjustment was observed. An important aspect of this research was the finding that subjects who were judged to be the best adjusted in various studies had high self-regard, "but their self-regard was not necessarily significantly better than that of the most poorly adjusted subjects". Wylie concluded that "we can see that the level of self-regard is far from being a valid indicator degree of pathology" (p. 217).

Although therapeutic claims on behalf of psychotherapy have sometimes been made on the basis of changes in self-concept scores, the omission of control groups is a crucial deficiency. In addition to the general inadequacies of the self-concept notion and its measurement (some of which have been enumerated above), it is necessary to draw attention to one further limitation. Dymond (1955) observed that a small group of 6 subjects who showed spontaneous remission and decided not to undertake therapy after being on a waiting list "appeared to have improved in adjustment, as measured from their self-description, about as much as those who went through therapy successfully" (p. 106). Their Q scores increased from 33 to 47.3 (significant at the 2% level). A comparison group of 6 apparently successfully treated patients (although there are some confounding variables here) showed changes from 34.8 to 48.3. The two groups were "not initially differentiable in terms of adjustment status at the beginning of the study". Instead of drawing what would appear to be the obvious conclusion, however, Dymond states that "no deep reorganisation appears to take place" (in the untreated patients). "The 'improvement' appears to be characterized by a strengthening of neurotic defences and a denial of the need for help" (p. 106). If Dymond's attempted explanation is correct, then presumably one would be entitled to conclude that a similar process occurs when the self-concept changes after psychotherapy. That is, can psychotherapy also be "characterized by a strengthening of neurotic defences"?

Further evidence that significant changes in self-concept occur without psychotherapy was provided by Taylor (1955). He found that subjects who were required to do self and self-ideal reports repeatedly showed the changes usually attributed to psychotherapy. The subjects showed an increase in the correlation between the descriptions of self and self-ideal, increased consistency of self-concept, and an increase in positive attitudes towards the self. Although these improvements are said by Taylor to be smaller in magnitude than those reported for cases of psychotherapy, this is doubtful. The comparisons which he made are between his experimental group of 15 subjects and 3 single case reports of disturbed patients. Either way his conclusion is consistent with Dymond's and interesting in itself: "significant increases in positiveness of self-concept, and in positive relationship between the self and self-ideal, may be valid indexes of improvement wrought by therapy, but increased consistency of self-concept is achieved so readily by self-description without counselling that it would seem a dubious criterion, especially when self-inventories or Q-sorts are used in conjunction with therapy".

Writers on the subject have expressed the following views. "When such tests are used in further research as if they had been carefully and adequately constructed, little can ensue but error and confusion. And such seems to be the case in self-acceptance research. Perhaps it is true that these tests are not yet used commonly in clinical settings where their inadequacies could lead to disservice to the client . . ." (Crowne and Stephens, 1961). Lowe (1961) cautiously concluded that "there is, in short, no complete assurance that the cognitive self-acceptance as measured by the Q-sort is related to the deeper level of self-integration that client-centred therapy seeks to achieve" (p. 331). Concluding her analysis of 29 research studies, Wylie (1961) said: "of course nothing can be concluded from these studies concerning the role of therapy in causing the reported changes" (p. 182).

Kellner (1967) has argued that the case for the effectiveness of psychotherapy is a sound one, and supports his conclusion by a reasonably detailed consideration of several studies. Many other studies are mentioned in passing and will not be taken up here, particularly as numbers of them are discussed elsewhere in this book. Here I will confine myself to those studies (other than with children or by counselling) on which Kellner bases the main force of his argument, but will not take up his discussion of those studies in which psychotherapy failed to produce results more satisfactory than the improvements observed in controls. It should be mentioned, however, that Kellner's attempts to explain the negative results which have frequently been reported are less than satisfactory. In his discussion of the Barron–Leary study, for example, he suggests that the untreated patients were probably less disturbed than their treated counterparts—despite evidence to the contrary contained in the study itself. On the other hand, his reservations about the use of various outcome criteria appear to be well grounded. He notes, for example, that MMPI scores are generally inappropriate and that "self-acceptance, if used as the only measure, is at present an inadequate criterion of improvement" (p. 345). He also notes a number of studies in which this type of assessment has failed to pick up therapeutic changes.

Kellner attaches significance to the 2 studies reported by Ends and Page (1957, 1959) in which they assessed the effects of various types of psychotherapy on hospitalized male alcoholics. As I feel that these studies fail to support the notion that psychotherapy is effective, it is necessary to consider them with care. Kellner describes the first of these studies in some detail and points out that 63 patients (out of an original group of 96) completed the programme: each of 4 therapists had 15 sessions with 4 different groups of patients. The methods of therapy were client-centred, psychoanalytic derivation, learning theory (an inappropriate designation), and, lastly, a social discussion group which served as control. In addition to the specific therapy, all patients participated in other presumably therapeutic activities during their stay in hospital. These included AA meetings, lectures, physical treatments, and so on. The outcome of therapy was evaluated by changes occurring in the self-ideal correlation. As Kellner points out, the MMPI which was used initially was discontinued, and the evaluation of therapy depended almost entirely on Q-sort analysis. He states that "$1\frac{1}{2}$ years after discharge from hospital the degree of improvement was judged by independent raters" (p. 345). He goes on to say that the "ratings $1\frac{1}{2}$ years after discharge showed a significant improvement in the 2 groups which had shown changes in the Q-sort". On the Q-sort analysis itself there were greater "reductions in the discrepancy between self and ideal in the client-centred group and in the psychoanalytic group". The second study (Ends and Page, 1959) is referred to briefly, and Kellner points out that although the self-ideal correlation again "discriminated significantly between treated patients and untreated controls", only the paranoia scale of the MMPI discriminated significantly. As Kellner regards MMPI scores as an unsatisfactory measure of outcome (and in any event these scores failed to show therapeutic changes) we will confine ourselves largely to a consideration of the other two measures, i.e. Q-sort analyses and follow-up ratings.

The Q-sort analyses are fairly complex and will be discussed at some length below. The follow-up data which appeared to have influenced Kellner's judgement of these studies are scanty and can be discussed fairly briefly. Ends and Page claim that the follow-up data show significant success for the psychotherapy groups but point out that the "results are by no means unequivocal" (p. 275). We might add that they are by no means clearly described. Although it is implied that follow-ups were carried out on 3 occasions, the results are all presented in a single table so that it is impossible to sort out the patients' progress at various stages. To make matters worse, it is not at all clear how the follow-ups were conducted or the data analysed. They say: "follow-up data from county welfare officers, from the hospital's own follow-up clinic, and from hospital admission records were analysed. The initial follow-up was made 6 months after discharge by county welfare officers using a standard interview form. The 1-year and $1\frac{1}{2}$-year follow-ups were made through the hospital follow-up clinic and hospital admission records" (p. 275). The results are presented in 5 categories but unfortunately the categories deal with different types of data and different time periods. For example, a rating of "greatly improved" was given when there was no evidence of further alcoholic episodes during the $1\frac{1}{2}$-year period. The rating of "possibly improved" was given when there was evidence of one or two brief episodes within the *first 3 months* following discharge and, "as far as could be determined no evidence of a reversion to the former pattern during the follow-up period". They define recidivism as "readmission to *the same* hospital for alcoholism" (our emphasis). It is in no way made clear that the patients were actually interviewed; in the context of the discussion it seems unlikely, but one cannot be sure. Secondly, it would appear that the follow-ups at the 1-year and $1\frac{1}{2}$-year periods were carried out by examining the information which happened to be present in the hospital's clinic and records. On the basis of their criterion for recidivism, it seems quite possible that their 1-year and $1\frac{1}{2}$-year follow-ups did not include the full sample—but only those patients who made contact with the hospital after discharge. If this is the case, the most that one can conclude is that patients who had undergone psychotherapy did not return to the same hospital and *not* that they were necessarily improved or abstinent. In view of their description of the composition of the category "possibly improved" there appears to be no certainty that the patients did not resume drinking after 3 months. As Kellner puts it, "fewer patients from the client-centred group had been readmitted to the hospital". His description of the follow-up procedure may, however, be slightly misleading. We cannot be sure that "the degree of improvement was judged by independent raters" at $1\frac{1}{2}$ years "after discharge from hospital".

In dealing with the first study, we feel that Kellner might have drawn attention to the extremely high defection rate—no fewer than 33 of the original 96 patients failed to complete the programme, i.e. a 30% loss rate. It is not stated whether the defections were more common in one or other of the groups, nor whether the defectors were comparable in initial status to the patients who completed the programme. Kellner might also have noticed that although Ends and Page excluded the MMPI data from their first study because "preliminary analysis revealed that physical and psychological treatment effects were confounded in the MMPI profiles", scores from the same test *were included* in the second study. The authors' inclusion of the MMPI data in the later study is doubly puzzling in view of their stated reason for excluding it, i.e. physical and psychological treatment effects were confounded. It is nowhere explained how they reached this conclusion or how they were able to decide that the Q-sort analysis "held such confounding to a minimum". In any event, they appear to have changed their minds in the second study.

Their Q-sort analyses are atypical and sometimes difficult to follow. Certainly their justification for using some of the analyses is doubtful. They carried out a large number of comparisons between different variations of the self and ideal-self correlations and found a number of significant "movement indexes". The client-centred group show 2 significant changes, the analytic group 3 significant changes, the learning theory group 2 significant changes and 2 negatives, and the controls 1 negative. A conclusion drawn from the comparisons is that the patients who received psychotherapy showed significant improvements, the control subjects showed little change and the "learning therapy" patients deteriorated slightly.

This conclusion appeared to be supported in their second study when they compared 28 patients who received twice as much client-centred therapy (i.e. 30 sessions) and 28 control patients who were simply assessed at the termination of the 6-week therapy period. In this comparison, however, the control patients were found to show some degree of improvement although not as large as the treated patients. One curious factor to notice here is that this second control group showed statistically significant improvements on 5 of the 8 comparisons, whereas the control group in the earlier study showed only 1 positive change and 1 negative change. The improvements observed in this second control group are, however, explained by Ends and Page as having been "gained minimally in self-acceptance only by a defensive manœuvre that appears to be unstable at the outset" (p. 12). The matter is made even more intriguing by comparing the control patients in the second study with the treated patients of the first study. The treated patients showed significant improvement on only 4 of the indexes. The major surprises, however, occur when the authors compare the patients who had 30 sessions of therapy with an additional control group of 28 patients who were simply re-tested after a 2-week wait period. "In general, figure 6 reveals that the control group made greater gains on 5 of the indexes than did the therapy group" (p. 23). Apparently these improvements represent "a defensive reaction" otherwise known as a "flight into health". This interpretation, we are told, is "supported by a wealth of clinical observation", and a "flight into health" is distinguished from "truly integrated therapeutic change". The difference in improvement scores between the treated and untreated groups is explained by the claim that group therapy "retards the flight into health" (p. 27). This flight into health apparently occurs "as a defence against self-examination and criticism" and on average occurs between the tenth and fifteenth therapy sessions. However, "this phenomenon seems to occur with or without therapy" (p. 24). We might note, incidentally, that if it occurs between the tenth and fifteenth therapy sessions the successful results obtained in the first study (in which 15 treatment sessions were given) appear to be fortunate.

On the MMPI results (considered in the first study to be confounding) the treated and untreated patients were found to produce significantly different results on only 2 of the 13 comparisons. The treated group showed significantly greater decreases in the paranoia scale, and the untreated patients showed significantly greater decreases in the Hy scale. We are also informed in the *second* study that the patients who received 15 treatment sessions, i.e. those in the first study, "demonstrated no significant change from pre- to post on any of the MMPI scales" (p. 14). Moreover, only one significant difference on the MMPI scales was observed between those patients who received 15 and those who received 30 treatment sessions. This is explained by Ends and Page on the grounds that the pre-treatment scores "suggest that the [first treated] group were somewhat healthier to start with as far as scale elevation is concerned. One would, therefore, expect less change on the MMPI scales simply because this group needed to move less, and, indeed, had less room in which to move since they began closer to the normal means for the scale" (p. 14). However, the same comment could be made about the untreated patients as they also show consistently lower MMPI scores than the patients who received 30 treatment sessions. We may even extend the argument to the analysis of the Q-sort data as the control group had a z score of 0.406 prior to treatment while the treated group had a score of 0.303.

Almost all of the conclusions reached by Ends and Page are doubtful. Conclusion number 6 is particularly misleading. They state that "the flight into health phenomenon occurs in those not participating in group psychotherapy. Following the inevitable collapse, those not receiving group therapy show no indications of reintegration in a therapeutic sense but instead recover by re-erecting a structure only superficially different from the initial one" (p. 29). As the so-called flight into health phenomenon (i.e. improved self-acceptance) was most clearly observed in the group which was re-tested after two weeks, it is hard to see how they can speak of an "inevitable collapse". This control group was *not* re-tested after the second week. It is not possible to say whether or not they "collapsed" or whether they "re-erected superficial structures" or showed no indication of "re-integration". On the contrary, when last tested they were showing considerable improvement.

It can be seen, then, that the studies by Ends and Page have serious shortcomings. The defection rate is extremely high and contains possible biasing factors. The selection of outcome measures, Q-sorts, and MMPI scores is unfortunate. The follow-up data are scanty and confounded. The Q-sort and MMPI scores suggest quite different conclusions. One of the untreated control groups shows considerable improvement after a 2-week wait period—greater than that seen in treated patients. Their exclusion of MMPI data from the first study is inconsistent. Their explanation of improvement in the untreated controls is unconvincing and, even if accepted, could be applied with equal significance to the improvements observed in some of the treated patients. As a great deal of time and effort was put into these studies it is a pity that the authors did not pay more attention to the accumulation of "hard" information such as status at follow-up determined by direct interview and by external informants. The total absence of follow-up data in the second study is particularly unfortunate. Overall, this research is devalued by implausible special pleading.

The study by Shlien *et al.* (1962) is frequently quoted as evidence in support of the effectiveness of psychotherapy. They compared the effects of unlimited client-centred therapy with time-limited client-centred therapy and time-limited Adlerian therapy. They included, in addition, 2 control groups. One control group consisted of normal people and can be dismissed as irrelevant. The other control group consisted of patients who requested therapy but did not receive it. These untreated controls were re-tested after 3 *months*. The sole criterion of therapeutic effectiveness was a self-ideal Q-sort.

The authors claimed to have demonstrated the effectiveness of psychotherapy and drew attention to the effectiveness of time-limited therapy. Apart from weaknesses in the experimental design, the authors reported their results in brief form and, regrettably, omitted vital details. For example, *all* of their results are presented as averages (mean or median?) and these are shown in the form of a graph. No actual figures are provided. It is nowhere stated what sort of patients they were dealing with. They do not indicate why the untreated group remained untreated. Nor do they state whether the allocation of patients to the treatment or no-treatment conditions was random—in the context of the report, it seems highly unlikely.

In regard to the experimental design used, one of the control groups is irrelevant. The other control group comprised untreated patients who may or may not have been re-tested at the follow-up period 12 months later. In any event they appear to have carried out the Q-sort on only 2 occasions as compared with 4 occasions for each of the treated groups. The sole criterion on which the effects of therapy are based is the Q-sort—generally agreed to be inadequate (e.g. Kellner, 1967). We are provided with no information about the psychiatric status of the patients either before or after treatment, nor are we told anything about their actual behaviour. In regard to the results themselves, the treatment groups appear to have shown substantial increases in self-ideal correlations. The untreated control group, on the other hand, shows a surprisingly unchanging course. Prior to treatment the self-ideal correlation for this group is precisely zero, and at the end of the 3-month waiting period it is still precisely zero. In the graph containing the results of the study they appear to be precisely zero at the 12-month follow-up period as well—but this may be misleading because it is by no means certain that they were re-tested at the follow-up occasion. In any event this remarkable stability is somewhat unusual. Ends and Page, for example, found that their 2-week waiting control patients showed an increase in self-ideal correlation of 0.25, i.e. they improved from 0.35 to 0.60 on re-test after 2 weeks. As mentioned earlier, other workers have found similar "spontaneous" changes in this type of correlation. In sum, the Shlien study will do as an exploratory investigation, but as evidence in support of the effectiveness of psychotherapy it is unconvincing.

Although Kellner's appraisal of the evidence appears to be over-optimistic, some of his comments on the problems of research into psychotherapy are well taken. In particular, he argues the case for increased specificity in a persuasive manner. Certainly, the treatment of a mixed bag of patients with a mixed bag of techniques is unlikely to further our understanding of the nature and possible effects of psycho-therapy.

Phipps Clinic Study

The by now well-known study of the effects of psychotherapy on psychiatric out-patients carried out at the Phipps Clinic has celebrated its tenth birthday, and the status of 34 of the original group of patients at the 10-year follow-up period has now been described by Imber *et al.* (1968). The patients were originally assigned at random to 1 of 3 forms of treatment: "individual psychotherapy, in which a patient was seen privately for 1 hour for once a week: group therapy, in which groups of 5-7 patients were seen for $1\frac{1}{2}$ hours once a week: and minimal contact therapy, in which the patient was seen individually for not more than one half hour once every 2 weeks" (p. 71). The treatment was carried out by second-year psychiatric residents who took no part in the evaluations of their patients. These evaluations took place at the end of 6 months of treatment and again 1, 2, 3, 5, and 10 years from the time of the initial treatment contact. A variety of assessments was carried out and the two main criteria were personal discomfort and social effective-ness. Significant improvements were observed in all 3 groups but some fluctuations occurred during the 10-year period, particularly among those patients who had minimal treatment. The main changes occurred within the first 2 years after treatment outset and, with some exceptions, tended to hold up at the 10-year follow-up period. As the authors remark, "it does seem somewhat improbable that differences consequent to a brief therapeutic experience a decade earlier should persist in such a striking fashion". Their argument is supported by a number of points, the most prominent of which is that some of the differences between treatments were absent at the 5-year follow-up period and then reappeared at the 10-year follow-up period. An overall evaluation of this admirably persistent investigation is complicated by fluctuations in the results and by an unfortunate lack of correspondence between the two major criteria. The omission of an untreated control group is understandable but unfortunate as it precludes any conclusions about the effect of psychotherapy *per se*. In view of the earlier discussion of possible events contributing to the spontaneous remission of neurotic disorders, the authors' findings on their patients' explanation of their improvements are interesting. "Although improved patients tended to associate their better current condition to a change in their socioeconomic situation or to their adaptation to general life circumstances, including symptoms, it cannot be determined whether psychotherapy fostered these changes or whether they occurred quite independently of the treatment experienced. In any event, it is clear that, in retrospect, patients conceive of improvement as a function of adjustment to their lot in life or to a change in external socio-economic circumstances" (p. 80). It is tempting to conclude from this study that psychotherapy was effective and that more psychotherapy was more effective (even when administered by inexperienced therapists). However, in view of the limitations of the study and the unclear outcome, I share the authors' caution. Although the results are inconclusive they do encourage the possibility that psychotherapy may be beneficial—even if it is provided in a brief and limited form by inexperienced therapists.

UCLA Study

Despite some unfortunate inadequacies in the analysis and reporting of their data, the study by Brill *et al.* (1964) contains interesting information. They carried out a long-term double-blind study of the use of placebos, prochlorperazine, meprobamate, and phenobarbital, "in conjunction with brief visits" in the treatment of 299 predominantly neurotic out-patients. The selection of patients was carried out in a systematic fashion, and on acceptance for the trial they were randomly allocated to 1 of the 3 drug treatments or to psychotherapy (given weekly for 1 hour's duration) or to a placebo control or to a no-treatment waiting list control. The authors conclude that the "patients in all 5 groups showed a tendency to improve, in contrast to a lack of improvement in the patients who were kept on a waiting list and received no treatment" (p. 594). They add that "the lack of any marked differences would suggest that neither a specific drug nor the length of the psychotherapeutic sessions was the crucial factor in producing improvement in this sample of patients" (p. 594). We may add that the patients receiving placebos did as well as the treated groups.

One of the most interesting findings was the resistance encountered by the investigators when the study was introduced and carried out. They comment on the "prejudice in favour of psychotherapy among patients and therapists" and point out that the "extent of the bias in favour of psychotherapy, even in beginning residents who had had very little experience with it, was quite startling" (p. 591). This was particularly surprising as "all of this took place at a time when, in fact, no one knew how effective or ineffective drug treatment was".

The effects of the treatment were assessed by a variety of procedures. The therapists rated the improvements on a symptom check list and a 16-item evaluation form. The patient was required to complete a similar item evaluation and one relative or close friend did likewise. In addition, a social worker carried out an evaluation of each patient—unfortunately the value of this information is limited by the fact that the valuation was carried out after the social workers had read the reports on each patient. Lastly, the patients were required to complete MMPI tests. The before and after profiles for each patient were drawn on the same profile sheet, and two independent psychologists sorted the profiles into degrees of improvement or lack of improvement. Although their evaluations agreed rather well ($r = 0.85$), their conclusions differed on one of the most crucial comparisons, i.e. whether the treated groups were improved to a significantly greater extent than the untreated controls.

It will be realized that this study required a great deal of effort and careful planning. It is particularly unfortunate, therefore, that the handling of the resulting information was inadequate. In fact it is extremely difficult to evaluate the information provided because they rarely give the actual figures obtained and rely almost exclusively on graphic presentations. The absence of basic information such as the means and standard deviations on the various measures before and after treatment is particularly serious. Matters are further confounded by their failure to give adequate descriptions of many of the assessment procedures employed. For these reasons and because they were almost exlcusively concerned with inter-group comparisons, we are not able to say with certainty whether any of the groups was in fact significantly improved. In order to reach a conclusion on this point one would need to have the means and standard deviations of the pre- and post-treatment assessment (subject, of course, to the usual tests of significance). The study is also limited by the unfortunately high rate of drop-outs—43.5% of the selected subjects either dropped out of the treatment or were not reassessed—or both. Despite some reassuring remarks made by the authors, there are indications that the drop-outs were somewhat different from the treated subjects. In their own words, "the drop-out group may be characterized as less intelligent, less passive, and more inclined to act out their problems" (p. 584). As the data for the groups are not provided, the matter remains in a degree of doubt except for the IQ scores, which are presented graphically. This shows the completed subjects to have a mean IQ of approximately 125. They were a group of superior intelligence and the drop-outs were of high average intelligence (approximately 115).

One of the major drawbacks to this study is the doubt which surrounds the degree of improvement, if any, shown by the treated and placebo groups. In some of the graphical presentations (e.g. fig. 5) they appear to have made "doubtful" to "slight" improvement. In other representations the changes seem to be slightly larger. Bearing in mind all these shortcomings, one can probably agree with the general conclusion reached by Brill and his colleagues to the effect that the treated (and placebo) groups showed slight improvement over a period of 1 year. They could detect no differences between the improvements registered by the 3 drug-treated groups, the placebo group, and the psychotherapy group. All of these groups, however, appeared to do better than the untreated waiting-list controls. Taken at face value, the main conclusion regarding the effects of psychotherapy would appear to be that it may have produced a slight improvement overall and this degree of improvement was neither smaller nor greater than that observed in patients who received placebos. The conclusion that psychotherapy is no more effective than an inert tablet can be avoided, however, by drawing attention to the shortcomings enumerated above. And one may also add that the psychotherapy was given for only 5 months and that much of it was conducted by trainee psychotherapists. As an attempt to evaluate psychotherapy the study must be regarded as inconclusive.

The information discussed so far is based on the condition of the patients at termination of treatment (mean duration 5.5 months). Koegler and Brill (1967) later reported their condition after a 2-year follow-up period. Their findings are striking: "The most marked improvement is in the rated status of the waiting-list (i.e. untreated) patients" (p. 77). At follow-up there were no significant differences between any of the groups. This suggests that at very best, treatment (by drugs, psychotherapy, or placebo) achieves improvement more quickly. The authors quote Jerome Frank's notion that ". . . the function of psychotherapy may be to accelerate a process that would occur in any case".

In regard to the question of spontaneous remissions, it will be recalled that Bergin was quoted as giving a zero rate for this study. In fact it is impossible to work out a percentage remission *rate* from the information given. The results are reported for the no-treatment waiting-list control group *as a group*, and while it is true that at termination they had shown relatively little change as a group, there is no way of determining whether any of the 20 remaining patients concerned (14 of the original 34 were lost) remitted spontaneously. Nevertheless, they caught up *within 2 years* and were then no different from the other groups of patients.

In the study by Greer and Cawley (1966), mentioned earlier, the relationship between treatment and outcome was also examined. It will be recalled that all of the patients were sufficiently ill to require in-patient care and they had the following types of treatment. Sixty-three received supportive treatment, 42 had physical treatment, 10 underwent leucotomy, 28 had psychotherapy, and 19 had psychotherapy combined with physical treatment. Thirteen patients received no treatment "as they remained in hospital less than 2 weeks and in most cases discharged themselves against medical advice". At discharge, the group of patients who had received psychotherapy "had a significantly more favourable outcome than the remainder". The mean outcome score for the 20 patients concerned was 1.96; the mean score for the 19 patients who had psychotherapy and physical treatment was 2.11 and the mean outcome for those 13 patients who received no treatment was 2.15. The worst outcome was recorded by the patients who underwent leucotomy, and they had a mean score of 2.60. Although this trend was seen to continue at "final outcome" (i.e. the follow-up), the difference between the patients who had psychotherapy and those who had no treatment was no longer significant. The significant advantage for the psychotherapy patients in relation to those who had received supportive treatment or physical treatment was maintained. The patients who had undergone leucotomy had the worst outcome of all, but their numbers were small. The more favourable outcome for psychotherapy patients when discharged from hospital may be misleading. Although no direct information is provided on the selection procedures in operation at the time of the patients' stay in hospital, there are significant indications that the patients who received psychotherapy were unrepresentative of the total patient sample. Greer and Cawley examined the significance of the factor of patient selection by carrying out some comparisons between the patients who received psychotherapy and the remainder. It was found that the psychotherapy patients "differed from the other group in several important respects". All of the patients receiving psychotherapy had a history of precipitating factors, and none of the 16 patients whose symptoms were regarded as being of life-long duration had received psychotherapy. In addition, a significantly higher proportion of psychotherapy patients were married and significantly fewer of them had an unfavourable pre-morbid personality. All of these features had previously been demonstrated by the authors to relate significantly to outcome, "so patients who had received psychotherapy would be expected to have had a more favourable prognosis, irrespective of treatment". They concluded that it would not be justifiable to ascribe the difference in outcome between the psychotherapy group and the rest of the sample to the effect of the particular treatment. Having noted that the patients selected for psychotherapy had a favourable prognosis irrespective of the particular treatment given, they go on to point out that "this argument does not necessarily demonstrate that psycho- therapy was *ineffective* in these patients. From the findings of the present study we are not entitled to draw any conclusions regarding the efficacy of psychotherapy" (p. 83). As we have already seen, however, the Greer–Cawley study contains a considerable amount of useful information on the course of neurotic illnesses. In regard to improve- ment rates and eventual outcome they unearthed a disconcerting finding. The correlation between immediate outcome (i.e. condition at discharge) and final outcome is very low—$r = 0.19$.

To sum up, it is disappointing to find that the best studies of psycho- therapy yield discouraging results while the inadequate studies are over- optimistic.

CHAPTER 6

THE NEGATIVE EFFECTS
OF PSYCHOTHERAPY

IT IS sometimes observed that patients get worse during or after a course of psychotherapy. This statement cannot be taken to imply that the psychotherapy *causes* the deterioration—any more than one can rashly presume that positive changes observed after psychotherapy are the result of that treatment. As a minimum, it is necessary in both cases to demonstrate that the positive or negative changes are greater than those which might be expected to occur in the absence of psychotherapy. Bergin (1970) has accumulated some reports on the putative deterioration effect in psychotherapy, but the quality of the evidence is not high. If, as seems to be the case, some patients do deteriorate spontaneously (i.e. in the absence of formal treatment), the occurrence of deterioration during or after psychotherapy is not adequate evidence that the therapy produced the negative changes. Before reaching a firm conclusion on such a serious matter it is essential to accumulate unequivocal evidence.

Over and above the clinical necessity of obtaining information about possible deteriorative effects of psychotherapy, this possibility is a central feature of the important argument about the so-called "average therapeutic effect". As noted earlier, there is fairly good agreement on the insufficiency of the available evidence concerning the positive effects of psychotherapy. Most writers also agree that the therapeutic claims made for psychotherapy range from the abysmally low to the astonishingly high and, furthermore, they would tend to agree that on average psychotherapy appears to produce approximately the same amount of improvement as can be observed in patients who have not received this type of treatment. The "average effect" argument is well stated by

Bergin (1967): "while some research studies reveal little difference in the *average amount* of change occurring in experimental and control groups, a significant increase in the variability of criterion scores appears at post-testing in the treatment groups. This conclusion was drawn from 7 (well-designed) psychotherapy outcome studies and was startling in that it directly implied that some treatment cases were improving while others were deteriorating, thus causing a spreading of criterion scores at the conclusion of the therapy period which did not occur among the control subjects. Evidently there is something unique about psychotherapy which has the power to cause improvement beyond that occurring among controls, but equally evident is a contrary deteriorating impact that makes some cases worse than they were to begin with: when these contrary phenomena are lumped together in an experimental group, they cancel each other out to some extent, and the overall yield in terms of improvement (in these particular studies) is no greater than the change occurring in a control group via 'spontaneous remission factors' " (Bergin, 1967, p. 184).

Before examining some of these findings in more detail, Bergin's qualification should be borne in mind. He states that the finding of increased variability at the end of treatment occurs "in these particular studies". It certainly cannot be said to be a universal observation.

Bergin's intriguing argument has numerous implications, but this discussion will be confined to what seems to be one of the most important aspects of his position. If he is correct, then one of the two conclusions given here must follow: either psychotherapy is capable of helping a lot of people and also making an approximately equal number of people worse—or very few patients are made worse by psychotherapy and an equally small number are improved by psychotherapy. As possible corollaries to these alternatives, we would have to add that either there is a large number of effective therapists and an equally large number of deplorable therapists or most therapists are relatively ineffective and also relatively harmless.

Turning now to the evidence presented by Bergin in support of his case, we must preface it by saying that he is perhaps a little uncritical in his use of the data. In particular he seems satisfied with the results obtained from a variety of tests and other measures which are either inappropriate or not known to be reliable or valid. One of the studies which Bergin quotes in support is that by Cartwright and Vogel (1960). He quotes from their paper as follows: "thus, as measured by the Q-score, adjustment changes, regardless of direction, were significantly greater during a therapy period than during the no-therapy period" (p. 122). Unfortunately, Bergin does not quote the very next sentence in the Cartwright paper. It reads as follows: "This was not true for the adjustment changes as measured by the TAT." Moreover, inspection of table 1 in the paper by Cartwright and Vogel shows that on both measures used in this study (Q-scores and TAT scores) the 22 experimental subjects showed greater variance in the *pre*-therapy period than during the therapy period itself. Although no figures are given, it is not likely that these differences are statistically significant. In any event, the study referred to by Bergin cannot be said to support the general case that therapy increases variance.

The next study to be considered is that of Barron and Leary (1955). It will be recalled that they carried out a reasonably well-controlled study of psychotherapy and found that it produced changes no greater than those observed in a non-treated group. In 1956 Cartwright re-analysed some of their data and concluded that although there was no difference between the two groups on average, "it seems that some therapy patients deteriorated to a greater extent than did the waiting list controls, while some therapy patients did improve significantly more than the controls". Unfortunately, as noted by Bergin, this effect "occurred only for individual and not for group therapy" (Bergin, 1966, p. 236). Even if this evidence were acceptable it still leaves unresolved the mystery of why the patients treated by group therapy, although showing the average effect, did *not* show an increased variance. On the face of it, the "average effect" observed in patients treated by group therapy *cannot* be accounted for by Bergin's hypothesis. This exception (and there are others) means that even if Bergin's hypothesis has merit, it cannot be a complete explanation of the so-called average effect of psychotherapy. There is a further complication. Barron and Leary in their first table (p. 242) presented the *pre-treatment* means and standard deviations for the three groups on the MMPI. On three of the subscales quoted by Bergin in support of his argument (F, K, Sc), the standard deviations in the group of patients who eventually received individual psychotherapy are greater than those observed in the no-treatment control group. Lastly, one may point out that the MMPI is far from being a satisfactory measure of putative psychotherapeutic changes.

A third piece of evidence offered by Bergin is taken from the study by Rogers and Dymond (1954). He says "it is even more fascinating that Cartwright himself participated in a study in which a similar phenomenon occurred . . . but it was never emphasized in proportion to its true import" (p. 236). Bergin calls this phenomenon "client-deterioration" and says that "a careful reading of the report indicates that of 25 therapy subjects, six, or 24%, declined in self-ideal correlation between pre-therapy and follow-up testing" (p. 236). Unfortunately, 7 of the *control* group subjects also showed a decline in self-ideal correlations (see Rogers and Dymond, table 2, p. 66). Moreover, if we examine the self-ideal correlations in the treated group we find that *at the end of treatment* only 2 of them have "deteriorated", and of these 1 subject moved from −0.12 to −0.17. The figures quoted by Bergin refer to the differences between pre-therapy correlations and *follow-up* testing. This is, of course, entirely permissible, but it is not consistent with Bergin's statement of the position—see above where he states "a significant increase in the variability of criterion scores appears at *post-testing* in the treatment groups" (my italics). If we are to place any reliance on these scores obtained from a self-acceptance Q-sort, we would have to conclude that the increased variance occurs *after* the termination of treatment, i.e. in the follow-up period. The number of patients who show such "deterioration" in the follow-up period is similar to that obtaining in the untreated control group.

Bergin also makes use of the study reported by Fairweather *et al.* (1960), which he says "yielded similar results". Bergin then quotes two sections from the report by Fairweather *et al.*, and these are, indeed, representative of their views but, nevertheless, somewhat misleading. As Fairweather says, the "control group *usually* had the smallest variance and 3 psychotherapy groups the largest" (my italics). However, the detailed results provided in this report are considerably more complex than this quotation indicates. One of the major determinants of the variance observed was the diagnostic category of the patients concerned and, furthermore, the mean variances for the control group subjects were often *larger* than those obtaining in the treated group. Regarding the question of diagnostic category, on all 5 of the major comparisons, the non-psychotic patients had smaller mean variances than the 2 other groups of patients (short-term psychotics and long-term psychotics). In regard to treatment groups, in every one of the numerous comparisons made, the control group (i.e. untreated) patients showed a larger mean variance than at least 1 of the treated groups. In some of the comparisons the non-psychotic control patients showed larger mean variances than *all* of the treated groups (e.g. self-report change scores shown in table 17, change scores for 5 ideal-sort scales in table 20). The results of this study are detailed and complex and repay inspection. They cannot be discussed at length here but it should be remembered that, in any event, the post-treatment ratings and psychometric scores were shown to have practically no relation to the clinical condition of the patient at the 6-month follow-up period.

Of the other studies discussed by Bergin, one deals with a brief (3-session) counselling study, another is the Cambridge Somerville report by Powers and Witmer (1951), and the last is the Wisconsin project by Rogers and his colleagues which will be discussed below. The Powers and Witmer report does in fact provide some support for Bergin's position. Other studies which run contrary to his argument include those of Gallagher (1953a, b), Cowen and Coombs (1950), and Baehr (1954). In all 4 the improvements are within the average range and more than 1 therapist was involved. In all of the studies, the variance on most or all of the outcome measures was reduced after treatment.

In sum, then, the evidence in support of Bergin's contention is scanty. At best, the "deterioration phenomenon" may provide a partial explanation for some of the so-called average psychotherapeutic outcome figures; it fails to provide a complete explanation. It has already been shown that even untreated patients show deterioration and, furthermore, such deterioration varies between different diagnostic groupings. The possibility that improvements and deteriorations in psychotherapy are determined, at least to some extent, by the effectiveness of the therapist is discussed by Bergin and has, of course, been the subject of extensive research by Truax and his colleagues. Lastly we should add that another determinant of therapeutic outcome (and probably the most important) is the selection of an appropriate and effective method of treatment for the particular disorder concerned.

The fact that Bergin's explanation is, at best, incomplete is, in a sense, a reassuring evaluation. Acceptance of his point of view as a complete explanation would imply one of the 2 following combinations mentioned above: psychotherapy is harmful as often as it is helpful and/or psychotherapy is conducted by therapists who are harmful about as often as they are helpful. Although this "helpful–harmful" hypothesis has been given a prominent place in the arguments of the Rogerian school of psychotherapy, it is fortunately not an essential feature. The major tenets of the Rogerian position were elaborated some years prior to the appearance of this argument.

CHAPTER 7

ROGERIAN PSYCHOTHERAPY

THE intensive and extensive growth of Rogerian psychotherapy has undoubtedly been one of the most important developments in the field of psychotherapy during the past decade. The necessary and sufficient conditions of therapeutic change were stated by Rogers (1957) with admirable clarity and lack of equivocation. He boldly attempted to specify "a single set of pre-conditions" which he felt were necessary to produce therapeutic change. These pre-conditions were, he argued, operative in *all* effective types of psychotherapy. The necessary and sufficient conditions which have received the greatest amount of attention all relate to the therapist's attitude, set, and/or behaviour. It is argued that constructive personality change is facilitated when the therapist is warm, emphatic, and genuine. Rogers claimed that "if one or more of these conditions is not present, constructive personality change will not occur".* He added that when these conditions are present in large measure, then the resulting personality change is more striking. One of the most radical aspects of Rogers's position was the argument that the treatment *technique* is not "an essential condition of

---

* The three "necessary and sufficient conditions" of effective therapy postulated by Rogers in 1957 are neither necessary nor sufficient. Their insufficiency is indicated by the recent addition of a fourth ingredient of self-exploration, by a fifth ingredient of "persuasive potency" (Truax *et al.*, 1968), and by the therapeutic failure of the Wisconsin project. The evidence presented by Truax and Carkhuff (1967) also shows that in numerous studies therapeutic changes were observed even though 1 of the 3 conditions was low. For example, "The Hopkins data, then, suggests that *when one of the three conditions is negatively related to the other two* [original italics] in any sample of therapists, then patient outcome is best predicted by whichever two conditions are most closely related to each other" (Truax and Carkhuff, p. 91). The 3 conditions may be facilitative but they are not necessary.

the therapy". He states that "the techniques of the various therapies are relatively unimportant except to the extent that they serve as channels for fulfilling one of the conditions". Rogers's theory is consistent—even to the extent of conceding that his own form of therapy is convenient but not essential. He says "in terms of the theory here being presented, this technique [client-centred] is by no means an essential condition of therapy".

He also adopts a radical view on the question of training. A successful therapist is a person who can provide high levels of the 3 therapist conditions, and "intellectual training and the acquiring of information" does not of itself produce a successful therapist.

In the first major outcome study reported by Rogers and his colleagues, a successful result was claimed (Rogers and Dymond, 1954). As discussed in Chapter 2, Eysenck argued that this claim cannot be sustained. In view of the fact that no suitable control group was provided and the "waiting control group" was not matched on the most crucial variable, the outcome of this study was inconclusive.

In 1967 Rogers and his colleagues produced a massive report on a treatment trial carried out on 28 schizophrenic patients, 16 of whom were treated. Although this study served the useful function of clarifying and refining the methodological procedures involved in a task of this magnitude, the *therapeutic* results were disappointing. Despite the intensive measurement and data analysis undertaken by the group, they were not able to confirm either of the 2 crucial predictions. The treated patients did not do better than the untreated controls. The patients who experienced high levels of the 3 crucial therapist conditions did not necessarily do better than those patients who experienced low levels of these conditions.

Although considerable progress was made in the development of the assessment techniques, some disconcerting findings also emerged. It was found, for example, that the scales for measuring 1 of the 3 conditions had a reliability which was so low that it precluded any useful result. It was also found that the therapist's assessment of their own behaviour differed significantly from that perceived by the patient or by an independent assessor. It was found also that the therapist variables thought to be important for neurotic patients did not apply to the schizophrenic group.

Obviously it is not possible to discuss the wealth of complex data in detail. It can be said with certainty, however, that this work by Rogers and his colleagues makes an important methodological contribution and is pertinent not only to Rogerian therapy but to all evaluations of psychotherapy. Nonetheless, the failure to obtain evidence of positive therapeutic effects in this intensive and carefully planned and executed study is a setback for Rogerian theory and therapy. Rogers's initial theory notwithstanding, the disappointing outcome of this study may well be attributable to what seems to have been an unwise selection of patients. For implicit and explicit reasons, schizophrenic patients seem to be less promising material for this type of treatment than other types of patient (e.g. personality problems).

Apropros the earlier discussion on the putative increases in variance observed after average therapy, the Wisconsin study provided scant support for this position. It is also worth noticing that in other studies reported by this group, treated patients do not always show increased variance. For example, Carkhuff and Truax (1965) in a study on the effectiveness of lay therapists showed that after treatment only 1 out of the 74 patients showed a deterioration. On the other hand, 12 out of the 70 non-treated control patients showed a deterioration. In this instance the effect of treatment was to *reduce* the variance.

Truax and Carkhuff (1967) have provided a coherent and important contribution to this subject. They describe and discuss in considerable detail the methodology involved in measuring the therapist conditions and they also assess the relations between the measures and across measures and therapeutic effect. In addition they propose a "fourth major ingredient of effective therapeutic encounters", namely the patient's depth of self-exploration. As the present work is concerned with the outcome of therapy, I will not examine their interesting accounts of how the therapeutic encounter can be assessed and quantified, or their analysis and recommendations for the training of therapists.

They discuss and describe a substantial number of experiments concerned with the reliability of therapist-condition ratings and the relationship between these measures and therapeutic outcome. Unfortunately, however, most of these studies lack adequate control groups. The control studies are few in number but they do in general encourage the view that satisfactory therapeutic conditions do facilitate therapeutic improvement. In view of the setback in the Wisconsin study mentioned above and for other reasons which will be gone into presently, a definitive affirmation of the effectiveness of this type of therapy must await further evidence.

Some of the reasons which account for this cautious attitude include the following. In the control studies, differences in the therapeutic conditions obtaining in various groups are sometimes extremely small. In the Dickenson and Truax (1966) study with college under-achievers, although they found significant differences between the groups receiving high and low conditions, an inspection of the ratings for the 3 groups shows that the *actual* differences are very slight. The mean ratings for the 3 groups were 13.2, 13.4, and 12.6 (presumably out of a possible total of 21). It will be seen that the differences are very slight despite the fact that group 3 received conditions that were (statistically) significantly lower than the other 2 groups. In spite of this very small difference in therapist conditions the outcome measures between the groups were surprisingly substantial. The study by Truax *et al.* (1966) on delinquent girls, although successful in the main, produced real differences that were comparatively slight (i.e. in the actual amounts of time out of institutions). Teasdale (1969), among others, has drawn attention to the need for independent confirmation of their findings by research workers outside the Truax–Rogers group. Many of the detailed difficulties which arise in evaluating the Rogerian approach are admirably discussed by Shapiro (1969), whose review is, in general, favourable. Among the many important points discussed in his paper, only a few will be mentioned here. Shapiro points out that the 3 scales contain ambiguities in terminology; the reliabilities of the scales are occasionally dangerously low; there is little evidence on the validity of the scales; the functional independence of the 3 therapeutic conditions is doubtful (see also the recent work by Muehlberg *et al.*, 1969, and Collingwood *et al.*, 1970). Discussing the outcome studies, Shapiro notes the presence of some contradictory and inconclusive results and suggests "that that simple hypothesis of positive association between conditions and outcome leaves much to be accounted for". He also draws attention to the inadequacies of the measures of change which are used in many of these studies—the shortcomings of some of the more popularly used

ones such as the MMPI and the Q-sort have already been discussed.

Cartwright (1968) is not convinced by Truax and Carkhuff. She has
pointed out, for example, that in the Truax and Wargo study on delinquent girls, even though there were differences in time out of institutions,
the groups did *not* differ on 4 out of 5 other measures. There were no
differences on anxiety, social relations, emotional stability, or self-ideal.
She also questions their assumption that the therapists were operating at
high levels of warmth and empathy. According to Truax, "this was
already established in previous research", but Cartwright doubts whether
"we are equally understanding and warm with all patients". She says,
"I would be very much surprised", and support for her scepticism has
been reported by Moos and Clemes (1967), who found clear evidence
of a patient–therapist interaction effect.

There are other difficulties. Even though Truax and Carkhuff present
some evidence on the connection between the therapist conditions and
degree of self-exploration, it has not been shown that there is a necessary
connection between self-exploration and therapeutic outcome. Perhaps
the most important limitation in all this work is their tendency to over-
emphasize the importance of therapist conditions and the consequent
lack of importance attached to treatment *technique* variables, the *nature*
of the patient's psychological difficulties, and, of course, the combination and interaction of these 2 determinants. The evidence on varying
rates of spontaneous remission in different diagnostic categories and the
differences in the natural history of various neurotic and other disorders
has been discussed above. Neglect of this information limits the value of
the Rogerian approach. The importance of selecting an effective
technique is demonstrated in the research on behaviour therapy (see
below). And in this connection it is worth noticing that the successful
results obtained with automated desensitization are a source of embar-
rassment to the Rogerian position (also, effective physical treatments,
drugs, etc.). Leaving aside the therapist conditions, it seems entirely
reasonable to suggest that the chances of a course of therapy proving
effective are determined to a very considerable extent by selecting the
appropriate treatment technique for the particular disorder. Starting
from this position it is far easier to then include the contribution made
by the therapist or, more accurately, the therapist conditions. It seems

entirely reasonable to expect (even in the absence of the work by Truax and Carkhuff) that therapists will differ in skill and effectiveness. The Rogerian work has served the important function of preparing the ground for an improved understanding of the way in which a therapist can facilitate the treatment process. Neglecting to consider the treatment technique and the psychological problem presented is likely to retard rather than facilitate our understanding of the contribution made by the conditions which the therapist offers. If, on the other hand, attempts were made to investigate these conditions in the context of the correct technique for the appropriate problem, we might look forward to some valuable findings.

It is suggested that this type of approach could be facilitated by recasting the Rogerian approach in terms of learning theory. Truax and Carkhuff have in fact made the initial steps in this direction by proposing that therapists who are high on the 3 conditions are potent positive reinforcers. Similarly, those therapists who are low on these qualities are ineffective or even negative reinforcers. They suggest that the potent therapist provides positive reinforcement of "approach responses to human relating", reinforcement of self-exploratory behaviour, the elimination of specific fears, and the "reinforcement of positive self-concepts and self-valuations" (pp. 151–5). Parts of this model bear some resemblance to Wolpe's (1958) view of non-systematic desensitization, which, he argues, can be used to explain the fact that most forms of therapy are capable of producing at least some therapeutic successes. Similarly, the Truax and Carkhuff model is congruent with some of the views put forward by Krasner (1962) on the reinforcing powers of a therapist.

If the Rogerian research proceeds from this model, it should be possible to bring about a fruitful integration with behavioural techniques, and the ensuing combination might be valuable.

CHAPTER 8

PSYCHOTHERAPY WITH CHILDREN

EYSENCK'S (1952) original evaluation of the effects of psychotherapy on adults was based on reports involving a gross number of 7293 patients. He concluded, of course, that the evidence failed "to prove that psychotherapy, Freudian or otherwise, facilitates recovery of neurotic patients". In 1957 Levitt carried out a similar examination of the data on the effects of psychotherapy on children and reached the same conclusion as Eysenck. He could adduce no evidence that psychotherapy with children is effective. Of the total number of approximately 8000 child patients included in his survey, roughly two-thirds were improved when treatment ended. However, this statistic was no greater than that obtained in children who did not receive psychotherapy; if anything, the treated group showed slightly fewer improvements. Levitt did observe, however, that time was a factor associated with improvement—the rate of improvement showing a negatively accelerating curve (Fig. 2).

Levitt (1957) calculated that the overall improvement rate for children who did not receive psychotherapy, even though it had been prescribed, was 72.5%. The comparison group chosen by Levitt was particularly apposite and consisted of "defectors" from treatment, i.e. patients from whom therapy had been recommended but not accepted or not completed. This comparison group provides a rough estimate of the spontaneous remission rate and was compiled from 2 reports in which disturbed children who defected from treatment were re-assessed 1 year later in the first study, and 8–13 years later in the other study. In evaluating the significance of the findings it is necessary to emphasize that Levitt has provided 3 independent types of evidence which demonstrate that the defector cases were equally as disturbed as those children who actually received treatment (Levitt, 1957, 1963). In his first study Levitt (1957) showed that the "defector cases and those who have had some treatment *do not differ on 61 factors*, including 2 clinical estimates of severity of symptoms and 8 other factors relating to symptoms" (my italics). In his second study, the treated and untreated children were compared on a 5-point severity scale by experienced workers. The mean severity rating of the treated group was 2.98

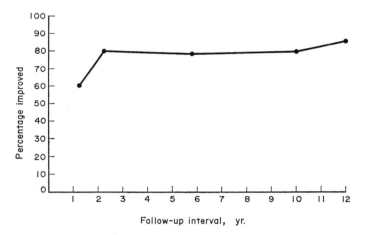

FIG. 2. The relationship between time and improvement in children's disorders—based on data compiled by Levitt (1957, 1963).

and that of the defector group was 3.02. Although other investigations have detected some differences between treated and defector groups, Levitt's (1963) criticisms of these studies appear to be well taken. In any event, his own findings cannot be ignored. Independent support for his conclusions has been provided by other workers, and one of the highest spontaneous remission rates ever recorded was that obtained by Clein (1959) in a study carried out at the Maudsley Hospital. Thirty-eight defectors were traced 3–5 years after applying for treatment. None of these children had received psychological treatment in the intervening period, but 86.9% of them were found to be improved or much improved at follow-up. It should be pointed out, however, that the composition

of this group of non-attenders was slightly atypical. Additional information about spontaneous improvements is provided by MacFarlane *et al.*
(1954) in their survey of the behaviour disorders of normal children.
They found that the frequency of most disorders declined with increasing age. Further data on the spontaneous remission of children's fears are
provided by Holmes (1938). O'Neal and Robins (1958) also conducted
a long-term follow-up of 150 patients who had attended a child guidance
clinic but not received treatment. These former patients did not display
more neurotic disturbances in adulthood than did the treated subjects.
They did, however, show more sociopathic disorders than did the controls.
It was found that those patients who had originally been referred for
extraverted disorders during childhood had failed to adjust satisfactorily
as adults. Other examples of spontaneous improvements in children
are discussed in Eysenck and Rachman (1965).

The 2 main points to bear in mind are the high rate of spontaneous
improvement and the possibility that "extinctions occurring naturally
during the life history of the individual should produce spontaneous
remissions in patients suffering from dysthymic conditions" (Eysenck,
1963). For the record, it should be mentioned that the overall percentage
of improvement recorded in the treated children who composed the
sample of Levitt's (1957) survey was 67%—and the estimated spontaneous improvement rate is 72.5%.

After completing this survey of the published reports, Levitt *et al.*
(1959) carried out a study of the effectiveness of a large and well-known
child guidance clinic in Illinois. They compared the status of 1000
patients at 5–6 years after acceptance or termination of treatment.
Their final, traced sample consisted of 237 treated children and 93
defectors. A careful examination carried out by interview and psychometric assessment revealed that there was "no difference at follow-up
between the adjustments made by treated and untreated child patients"
(p. 348). The apparent failure of treatment to alter the prognosis of these
children must be treated with reserve, however, as approximately half
the children who received treatment were seen by inexperienced
therapists.

In 1963 Levitt extended his original appraisal of the evidence by
including 24 newly published reports. This evidence brought no comfort. He concluded that there still "does not seem to be a sound basis

for the contention that psychotherapy facilitates recovery from emotional illness in children". Once again, the overall recovery rate showed that 2 out of 3 children are improved when treatment ends— approximately as many as can be expected to recover without treatment. In response to the well-taken criticisms of Eisenberg, Levitt's second appraisal contained analyses of the results of treatment *within* diagnostic groups. He reached the tentative conclusion that "the improvement rate with therapy is lowest for cases of delinquency and antisocial acting-out, and highest for identifiable behavioural symptoms like enuresis and school phobia". This tentative ranking of recovery rates within diagnostic groupings is interesting in the light of Eysenck's prediction mentioned above, and it has received indirect support from a variety of sources. As will be shown later, it seems that Levitt's estimate of a 65% overall improvement rate in what he classifies as "psychosis" is very probably a high estimate based on a widely embracing use of this diagnostic term—certainly this recovery estimate could never be matched by British statistics. Prevailing clinical practice in Britain restricts the use of this diagnostic category to an extremely small, particular group. Levitt's approximate ordering of other types of disturbance is consistent with, for example, the work of Morris *et al.* (1954), Morris *et al.* (1955), Warren (1965), and Turner *et al.* (1970).

The gloomy outlook for children who develop clearly psychotic disorders is shown in the work of Rutter (1965) and Eisenberg (1957) among others. At present, neither psychotherapy nor any other form of therapy is apparently capable of influencing the prognosis of this disorder to a significant extent. Although some promising developments are taking place (see Chapter 11), the most rational and helpful course to take with these children is to provide suitable psychological, educational, and social rehabilitation. In his important work on the subject, Rutter (1965) was forced to conclude that "there was little evidence that psychotherapeutic treatment of the child influenced prognosis". Similarly, Eisenberg (1957) found that "our follow-up study fails to reveal any correlation between formal psychiatric treatment and clinical outcome". Eaton and Menolascino (1967) concluded that "there was no correlation between therapy and clinical improvement". Creak's (1963) follow-up study on 100 children also failed to provide evidence for a positive effect of therapy. Davids *et al.* (1968) carried out a follow-up study of 27 severely disturbed children who had required in-patient psychiatric care; of these, 10 had been diagnosed as suffering from childhood schizophrenia. In addition to the general clinic care provided for each child, they were all seen in individual psychotherapy sessions on a regular basis. They found that there was a "lack of association between treatment variables and outcome variables", and this was true "not only for the psychotic children but for the entire sample of disturbed children" (p. 473). In their discussion they emphasize the generality of their finding that "treatment variables (especially conventional psychotherapy) seem to bear little relationship to subsequent adjustment". They go on to say that "these findings suggest that the main factors determining outcomes of psychiatric treatment may not be the specific therapies employed, but the kinds of symptoms and behaviours the patients bring with them to the treatment setting".

This conclusion receives support from a variety of sources. Barbour and Beedell (1955) carried out a retrospective analysis of the effects of child guidance clinic treatment. Five years after the termination of treatment they found that there was a general trend towards improvement in the majority of cases, but that there was no difference between the 65 patients who had received individual psychotherapy and the 178 who had had no treatment whatever. They also observed that there was no relationship between the amount of treatment received and the eventual outcome. Although his follow-up study of disturbed adolescents was not concerned with treatment variables, Warren (1965) also found that there was a general trend towards improvement. He noted in addition, as have several other workers in different contexts, that the patients with neurotic disorders fared best. They were followed by the patients with mixed disorders, and those with conduct disorders did less well than these 2 groups. He also found that the psychotic patients had by far the worst outcome. Along similar lines, Hare (1966) found that neurotic patients did best, and those with conduct disorders had a relatively unfavourable prognosis.

Eisenberg and his colleagues (e.g. Cytryn et al., 1960), recognizing that there were "no convincing studies that established the permanence of change resulting from intensive psychotherapy", have made several attempts to evaluate the effects of various treatment programmes. In the

1960 study they assessed the effects of brief (± 5 sessions), supportive psychotherapy. Having obtained indications that this brief intervention produced beneficial results, they subsequently conducted a controlled study on 83 neurotic children. They found that the neurotic children showed the greatest change and the antisocial children practically no improvement. Eisenberg *et al.* (1965) compared brief psychotherapy (5 sessions of supportive work) with the effects of a single consultation. They found that the immediate effects of the treatment intervention (judged after 8 weeks) were beneficial and significantly greater than those obtained only on consultation. As controlled studies of psychotherapy in childen are extremely rare, this encouraging result is welcome. However, the conclusion cannot be accepted without reserve. The psychiatric assessments of the children were carried out by their therapists, and "thus rating bias could not be excluded". Secondly, the actual differences between the groups, although significant on some of the measures (but not all), were small. The therapist's assessment was to some extent confirmed by ratings obtained from the children's teachers. Once again, although the differences between the two groups are statistically significant, the actual figures (i.e. degree of clinical improvement) involved are slight. Moreover, the teachers' ratings are expressed as a total score "above the median" or "below the median". In fact this single figure is a composite of the ratings of 5 different categories of behaviour, and there is no description of the scale or its validity and reliability. Nor is it made clear to what extent the children were above or below the median. Lastly, no follow-up data are provided.

In the absence of suitable evidence, however, it is necessary to make maximum use of the few controlled studies which have been reported. If we put the most favourable interpretation on the Eisenberg study we might conclude, with some reserve, that brief supportive psychotherapy may be effective in the short term at least. It is not possible to say, however, whether the therapeutic intervention merely accelerated an ongoing process or whether it effected a change in the "natural course of events". It should be borne in mind, however, that the results obtained in this study were achieved by brief and supportive therapy—a far cry from intensive psychotherapy extending over several years. The argument in favour of brief intervention is supported by Hare (1966), who reported favourable results in a non-controlled study.

Despite a considerable investment of time and effect, Dorfman's (1958) experimental evaluation of the effects of client-centred child therapy unfortunately adds little to our assessment of the effects of therapy. Although a control group was employed in this study, the maladjusted children were matched with *normal* children—a curious design fault similar to that in the Rogers and Dymond (1954) study on client-centred therapy with adults. Moreover, the effects of treatment rested entirely on psychometric measures, and here the author is refreshingly self-critical: "Perhaps the greatest shortcoming of the present study is the lack of behavioural criteria of changes attributable to therapy. Improvements noted on psychological tests do not necessarily mean better interpersonal relations, freer use of intellectual capacities, more mature behaviour, or the achievement of other goals generally implicit in the process of therapy. To measure these requires observation of the child outside the therapy and testing situations, which was unfortunately beyond the scope of this investigation" (p. 17). She goes on to say that the inclusion of behavioural criteria is "particularly important in view of the report by Teuber and Powers . . . in a large-scale study of therapy outcomes among pre-delinquents . . . they found no difference in later delinquency of therapy and control cases, despite the optimistic views of clients and therapists". Even the psychometric differences between the treated and (normal) control group are difficult to interpret, and preclude any firm conclusion. The Rogers test is a highly doubtful measure of therapeutic effectiveness. In the first place, the scores on the main scale of this test did not differentiate between the maladjusted patients and the normal controls *prior* to treatment. In other words, the validity of this test as a measure of maladjustment is debatable. Secondly, Fleming and Snyder (1947) found a poor correspondence between the Rogers test and other indices of improvement. Lastly, Seeman and Edwards (1954) found that the Rogers test results moved in "a direction contrary to expectation". In their study, the Rogers tested showed a deterioration in adjustment in a group of treated children even though they had made good educational progress and showed improved adjustment on another test (the Tuddenham test).

In their controlled comparison study on the treatment of enuresis, De Leon and Mandell (1966) found that the effects of individual psychotherapy were indistinguishable from the changes observed in a no-treatment control group. These two groups were compared with a third sample consisting of 36 children who were treated by the bell-and-pad conditioning method. The percentage success rates for the 3 groups were as follows: conditioning ($n = 56$) 86%; psychotherapy ($n = 13$) 18%; untreated control ($n = 18$) 11%. A strikingly similar result was obtained in an independent study by Werry and Cohrssen (1965). Their 21 psychotherapy patients had 6–8 individual treatment sessions. They also treated 22 patients by conditioning and had a non-treated control group of 27 cases. The cured or greatly improved success rate for the 3 groups was as follows: controls 10%; psychotherapy 20%; conditioning 60%. The results in the unchanged/worse category were: controls 70%; psychotherapy 70%; conditioning 20%. In an extensive review on the subject of enuresis, Lovibond and Coote (1970) concluded that while the evidence does not "permit the conclusion that psychotherapy *per se* is effective in the treatment of nocturnal enuresis", they were unable to locate any supporting evidence, and inserted a caution about recommending psychotherapy for this disorder (p. 380).

In similar vein, Werry and Sprague (1970) reviewed the literature on hyperactivity and concluded that "the utility of psychotherapy, whether individual, group, or family has not yet been established as a treatment of hyperactivity" (p. 412).

Humphery (1966) made an ambitious attempt to compare the therapeutic effectiveness of psychotherapy and behaviour therapy. The patients for these 2 groups, and a non-treated defector control group, were drawn from 2 clinics in south-east England. There were 17 patients in the psychotherapy group, 20 in the behaviour therapy group, and 34 controls. All of the treatment was carried out by Humphery, but his assessment of treatment outcome was supplemented by teacher ratings and by an independent, blind evaluation carried out by 1 of 2 consultant psychiatrists.

Almost all of the treated patients showed at least a "slight" improvement. Both forms of treatment produced greater improvement than that observed in the controls, 23 out of 34 of whom showed some slight improvement. The amount of improvement associated with the behaviour therapy was greater than that seen after psychotherapy. The differences in improvement between the groups were maintained at the 9-month follow-up examination. Although the group of patients who received behaviour therapy was only marginally more successful than those groups who received psychotherapy, there was a striking difference in the economy of the 2 methods. The improvements in behaviour therapy required only half as much treatment time (mean of 17 sessions) as did the group receiving psychotherapy (mean of 31 sessions).

The major findings can be summarized as follows. Both forms of treatment produced better outcomes than were seen in the non-treated controls—but these patients also showed at least slight improvements (66% of all cases). There was a slightly superior result obtained with behaviour therapy when compared with psychotherapy. Behaviour therapy was much more economical in time and effort than psychotherapy. The differences between the groups observed at termination of treatment were maintained at the 9-month follow-up period.

In view of the intrinsic difficulties in this experimental design and some unforeseen difficulties, the results will require confirmation. All of the treatment was carried out by the same therapist, and while he attempted to assist all of the patients (and as has been shown, his attempt was largely successful), the possibility of bias cannot be ruled out. Clearly, a replication of this finding in a study employing several therapists would be most helpful. A second difficulty with the study is that it proved impossible to ensure that the 2 methods of treatment were sufficiently different at all times. The study was carried out at a time when the behavioural techniques for helping children were undergoing development and, in a number of instances, *ad hoc* procedures had to be employed. In the main, however, the emphasis was on desensitization treatment—at that time, the contingency management of behavioural disorders in children had not reached the stage where it could be translated adequately into clinic practice. The experimental design was based on random allocation to the treatment groups and, as ill luck would have it, the children in the behavioural group were on average more severely disturbed (pre-treatment) than the psychotherapy cases. Another problem arose during the analysis of the data when it became evident that there were differences between the independent assessors—or, possibly, between the 2 clinics which they serviced. In any event it appears that the 1 independent assessor was somewhat lenient in his ratings whereas the other was severe. The therapist's own ratings were, without exception, found to lie between those of the 2 independent assessors. Subject to confirmation, this experimental trial suggests that both forms of treatment may be capable of effecting improvements in disturbed children. These benefits appear to have been greater than those which occur spontaneously in untreated patients. The behavioural techniques are slightly superior to psychotherapy and are more economical.

One other hopeful advance has been made by Chess and her colleagues (Thomas et al., 1968). The appeal of their work lies chiefly in the rational and systematic approach which they have adopted in an endeavour to produce effective therapeutic procedures. They are attempting to apply the findings which are emerging from their longitudinal study of temperament and behaviour to the "treatment" of behaviour problems in children. The treatment mainly consists of direct guidance of the parents supplemented by drugs or other measures where necessary. The early results, obtained with economical effort, are encouraging. It is to be hoped and expected that, with further development, this approach will be integrated with behavioural techniques, particularly those of contingency management (e.g. Ullmann and Krasner, 1965). The combination should prove fruitful.

It would seem to be the case that not all therapeutic interventions are futile. There are indications that even brief, supportive psychotherapy or parental guidance may induce therapeutic changes (or simply accelerate natural process of recovery?). There is also the possibility that recovery may be induced or accelerated by behavioural treatment and, conceivably, by certain types of psychotherapy. These are encouraging signs but they should be seen in the context of a high spontaneous recovery rate among maladjusted children and repeated failures to demonstrate putative therapeutic effects (e.g. Levitt's evaluations). The necessity for maintaining an adequate perspective on therapeutic interventions in childhood disorders is demonstrated in an epidemiological study by Shepherd et al. (1966). They carried out a comparison between a group of 50 children attending child guidance clinics and a group of children matched by age, sex, and behaviour. "The matched group were taken from a representative 1-in-10 sample of supposedly healthy children attending local authority schools in the county of Buckinghamshire. The results indicate that referral to a child guidance clinic is related as much to parental reaction as to morbidity, and that approximately two-thirds of both groups had improved over a 2-year period" (p. 48). In this study, as in others, they were unable to find any difference in the number of clinic attendances of the improved or deteriorated children.

In discussing their results they refer to a comment made by Ryle to the effect that "for each child referred to child guidance clinics there are 5, equally disturbed, not referred". The Shepherd study showed that the chief reason for referral to a guidance clinic was the reaction of the parents to the child's behaviour. The authors draw 2 important conclusions from their evidence: "the most obvious inference . . . is the existence of a large pool of morbidity in the community", and "many so-called disturbances of behaviour are no more than temporary exaggerations of widely distributed reaction patterns". They go on to say that "the transient nature of these reactions is demonstrated by the tendency to spontaneous improvement in the untreated children".

The value of epidemiological studies of this type is self-evident and, as mentioned earlier, further details about the course of different types of behavioural disorder are needed. Roughly one-third of the treated and untreated groups were still in difficulty at the 2-year follow-up period. From the therapeutic point of view, one would need to know why these problems did not improve spontaneously and, of course, whether it is possible to *induce* beneficial changes by any form of treatment. For the majority of children, the two-thirds who recover within 2 years, therapeutic interventions may yet serve a purpose—albeit a somewhat different one from that which underlies most of the prevailing types of therapy. In these cases of spontaneous recovery, therapy may accelerate the natural restorative processes and/or provide comfort for the child (and family) while the improvements in adjustment are allowed to occur.

CHAPTER 9

PSYCHOTHERAPY
WITH PSYCHOTIC PATIENTS

ALTHOUGH few psychotic patients actually receive interpretive psychotherapy, the suitability of such treatment has been debated for nearly 50
years. A considerable amount has been written on the subject and much
advice has been offered. In their substantial text on schizophrenia,
Bellak and Loeb (1969) described over 20 recommended forms of
treatment. There are wide differences between the various "schools of
thought" and even within schools. The more prominent "schools"
include Freudian, Kleinian, Jungian, Sullivanian, direct analysis, and
existential analysis. Surveys of current thinking on the subject are given
by Boyer and Giovacchini (1967), Auerbach (1961), and Bellak and
Loeb (1969). Depending on one's optimism or scepticism, one can
regard the profusion of ideas on the subject as reflecting a healthy state
of affairs or deplorable chaos. Rosenthal (1962) represents the sceptical
point of view and lists some of the methods which have been recommended for the treatment of psychotic patients. "To name a few: plan
emotional contact on a conceptual basis; interpret dependence rather
than hostility; use the patient's own language; give direct support, talk
about the weather, read children's stories to the patient, offer him
cigarettes, make no demands, ask no questions, and expect no responses; explain to the patient that he is ill and tell him the meaning of
his symptoms without arguing; provide symbolically all the wish-
fulfilments demanded by the patient's unconscious; establish a mother–
child relationship with him, without its possessive, narcissistic elements;
address one's self to the patient as an adult rather than as a child; make

deep, surprising, and shocking interpretations; assert an authoritarian, restraining role; facilitate a narcissistic object relationship and provide gratification of the patient's instinctual drives; foster repression; make external reality simple and attractive; reach out to the patient; work through the problem of hospitalization; use non-verbal techniques; focus on the person rather than the illness; encourage non-conformity."

Notwithstanding all this advice, the sample of English senior psychiatrists who gave their opinions in a survey conducted by Willis and Bannister (1965) did not favour the treatment of psychotic patients by deep psychotherapy. Only 6.8% of them considered Freudian psychotherapy to be a suitable treatment for schizophrenia, that is exactly the same percentage who still felt that insulin-coma treatment was appropriate. However, 56.6% recommended supportive individual psychotherapy, by which they generally meant reassurance, advice, and sympathetic listening. A similar survey of Scottish psychiatrists revealed that only 25% of them felt individual psychotherapy to be suitable for psychotic patients (Mowbray and Timbury, 1966).

In assessing the effectiveness of any form of psychotherapy, one has, of course, to bear in mind the spontaneous remission rate for the disorder under consideration. There have been many accounts given of the natural course of psychotic illnesses, but during the past few decades it has been impossible to obtain information about patients who have received no care whatever. Current opinion has it that the spontaneous remission rate in schizophrenia, for example, varies between 20 and 40% (e.g. Lindelius, 1970), with notable differences between those illnesses which have an acute or insidious onset. In 1966, Wing reported a 5-year outcome study in early schizophrenia and found that "about one-quarter of schizophrenic patients were still severely ill 5 years after first admission and another one-quarter were handicapped by less severe symptoms". On the other hand, "half of first-admitted patients have an excellent 5-year follow-up prognosis and require little attention from psychiatric after-care or rehabilitation services. Half of the patients in this sample were discharged from hospital within 13 weeks, and although no psychotherapy was apparently provided, the majority were given drugs. The sample consisted of 111 patients admitted for the first time in 1956. Kind (1969) estimated that the spontaneous remission rate for schizophrenia varies between 20 and 40% with differences occurring between acute and slow onset illnesses. The bad prognostic factors include slow onset and poor pre-morbid personality. Slater and Roth (1969) provide similar estimates and note "that most spontaneous remissions" occur "during the first 2 years of illness; after 5 years, they become negligible" (p. 311). Approximately 45% remit within 2 years, but after that the remission rate declines sharply.

In considering these spontaneous remission rates, and therefore the effects of treatment as well, one has to bear in mind that there are substantial differences in classification across different countries. For example, Cooper (1969) has shown that the diagnosis of schizophrenia is applied far more widely in the United States than it is in Britain. Many patients who in Britain would be considered to have a personality disorder would, in the United States, be diagnosed as schizophrenic. Another important difference was found in the diagnosis of "manic-depressive". Although quite commonly used in Britain, this diagnosis is rarely made in the United States. These differences in diagnostic practices are, to put it mildly, inconvenient. A consequence of differing national practices is that one has to exercise a great deal of care in drawing conclusions about research conducted in different countries. As virtually all of the outcome studies on the treatment of psychotics by psychotherapy have been carried out in the United States, the problem does not arise in a serious form in this chapter. Nonetheless, any evaluation of treatment effects in the future should take these diagnostic differences into account. Another factor which is of some importance in assessing the value of treatment in psychoses arises from the fact that severely ill patients tend to show some response to almost any increase in stimulation—whether it comes in the form of a specific therapeutic intervention or whether it consists of non-specific changes in their general care (e.g. the total push programmes described by Myerson, 1939). The value of "social treatments" of patients with chronic illnesses is admirably summarized by Wing (1968), who also reported an investigation of the response of chronic schizophrenic patients to social stimulation in which it was shown that an increased stimulation produces favourable therapeutic changes (Wing and Freudenberg, 1961). They also point out that patients who receive minimal stimulation tend to deteriorate: "controlled trials specifically testing these measures (particularly group psychotherapy) have been carried out very infrequently, and those which have been published have not yielded very positive results. One very common finding, however, has been that deterioration occurs in the control group which has not received treatment, even when no improvement has occurred in the experimental group" (p. 311). Their findings and observations underline the necessity for including an appropriate control group whenever a treatment for psychotic conditions is investigated, and it should be ensured that the control group receives the same amount of stimulation as the experimental group.

In his published works Freud (1932, 1940) was pessimistic about the possibility of treating psychotic disorders by psychoanalysis. He felt that the patient's inability to develop a transference precluded the development of a beneficial therapeutic relationship, and he also felt that if the analysis was successful in removing the patient's presumed defences, the overall result might be undesirable. According to Brill (1944), Freud became a little more optimistic in his later years and felt that "in time we would develop a psychoanalytic therapy for the psychoses". In view of the poor results reported by no fewer than 5 psychoanalytic institutes, Freud's early misgivings appear to have been well judged. Furthermore, his pessimism about the value of psychoanalytic treatment appears to be shared by the majority of psychiatrists in this country.

In his 1941 review of the effects of psychoanalytic treatment, Knight found that in all the institutions covered by his survey, psychotic patients came off least well—"psychoses [come] last with 25% success" (p. 439). At the Berlin Psychoanalytic Institute, 61 psychotics were accepted for treatment, 32 broke off treatment, and only 7 were considered to be much improved or cured. At the London Psychoanalytic Clinic they recorded only 1 success out of 15 cases. At the Chicago Institute, 2 successes out of 6 cases. At the Menninger Clinic they claimed 14 successes out of 31 cases, and Hyman and Kessel reported 7 failures out of 7 attempts. Knight's composite improvement rate over all institutes showed only 22 successes out of 120 cases—probably as many as might be expected to improve without treatment. More recently, Heilbrunn (1966), reporting on the results of psychoanalytic treatment with 173 patients, confirmed the poor results with psychotic patients. "The results were uniformly negative for the patients with psychotic reactions and personality pattern disturbances" after considerable psychoanalytic treatment.

Despite the dismal statistics and the pessimistic views of the majority, a small number of therapists have shown persistence in attempting to treat psychotic patients by means of psychotherapy.

Before considering the studies which employed control groups, the results of Saenger's (1970) recent actuarial study should be mentioned. He found that among patients with schizophrenic symptoms "considered highly suitable for psychotherapy, the net improvement rate for untreated (21%) and treated (17%) was about the same" (p. 45).

May and Tuma (1965) carried out a study on 100 first-admission schizophrenics. Four types of treatment were compared with a control procedure consisting of basic hospital care: one group received drugs only, the second group received psychotherapy, the third group a combination of drugs and psychotherapy, and the fourth group received ECT. The patients who received psychotherapy had a minimum of 6 months' treatment consisting of not less than 2 hours per week, and the treatment was supervised by a psychoanalyst experienced in treating schizophrenics. Four outcome measures were employed, and a 3-year follow-up was carried out. It was found that the patients who had drugs did significantly better than the control patients, but there was no difference between those who received psychotherapy or control treatment (basic hospital care). They did not differ on any of the 4 outcome measures, including length of time in hospital, nor did they differ at the 3-year follow-up. Indeed, the control and psychotherapy patients had both spent an equivalent amount of time in hospital: controls 374 days and psychotherapy patients 395 days. In the Wisconsin project carried out by Rogers *et al.* (1967), discussed in Chapter 7, it will be recalled that psychotherapy did not produce significantly better results than were obtained in non-treated control patients. In a comparison trial in which the experimental and control patients were well matched, Powdermaker and Frank (1953) were unable to find support for the hypothesis that psychotherapy was beneficial. A large number of statistical comparisons were made between the control and experimental group patients, including discharge rates, trial absences, etc., but they found very few differences between the groups, and those which did emerge could not and were not interpreted as providing evidence of the effectiveness of psychotherapy. Another failure was reported by Satz and Baraff (1962). Two groups of non-paranoid non-chronic schizo-phrenic patients ($n = 8$ in each group) received 13 hours of intensive occupational therapy. In addition, the psychotherapy group received 2 hours of group psychotherapy for 10 weeks. The effects of psycho-therapy, as measured by self-ideal correlations, "were negligible". In fact, the controls showed a large but non-significant superiority. It can, of course, be argued that this experiment was not a fair test of the effects of therapy as the amount of treatment given, 20 hours, was small. In addition, their use of the Butler–Haig Q-sort was ill-advised as it provides a doubtful measure of therapeutic change.

Cowden et al. (1956) compared the effects of psychotherapy and drug treatments, alone and in combination, with routine hospital care as a control baseline. Thirty-two chronic schizophrenic patients were ran-domly assigned to 1 of the 4 groups, and the treatment experiment continued for 6 months, with group psychotherapy given for 3 sessions of 1 hour per week. The majority of outcome measures showed no difference for the treated or untreated groups, but there was 1 measure on which the patients who received psychotherapy and drugs were superior to the other treatment groups. This was a measure of specific types of behaviour (e.g. fighting), but the groups were grossly different prior to treatment. The measures on which no differences were found between groups included 2 rating scales and 4 psychological tests. Kraus (1959) tested the effects of twice-weekly group psychotherapy in chronic schizophrenic patients. The effects of the treatment, which were carried out for 3 months, were assessed by comparison with patients in a matched control group who received routine hospital care. The main outcome measure was the MMPI, and it failed to discriminate between the treated and untreated groups. In addition, blind ratings by a psychiatrist failed to reveal any differences between the treated and untreated patients although the ward physician—who was aware of the identity of the treated patients—rated the experimental patients as being substantially better than the control patients. Once again, it can plausibly be objected that the amount of treatment provided was not sufficient.

In their study of psychotherapeutic effectiveness, Fairweather et al. (1960) advisedly took into account differences in diagnostic categories.

The main aim of their study was to determine the effects of individual or group psychotherapy on neurotic short-term psychotic and long-term psychotic patients. No fewer than 7 major outcome measures were used on the total of 96 patients involved (this includes a non-treated control group). Their findings are dominated by the effect of the major variable, i.e. diagnostic category, which accounted for most of the differences obtained. In the main, it was found that neurotic and short-term psychotic patients did best while the long-term psychotics had an unfavourable outcome, and there is even a suggestion that they did *better* without treatment. "It is evident that the major contributor to the significant interaction is the differential response of the diagnostic groups to all three psychotherapy treatments compared with the control" (Fairweather *et al.*, 1960, p. 14). Their failure to demonstrate significant treatment effects on the MMPI, Q-sort, or TAT is partly compensated for by a suggestion that the treated groups were doing slightly better at the 6-month follow-up. In fact, one of the most interesting findings in this study was the absence of any association between test-score indicators of treatment outcome and adjustment at follow-up. Closer inspection of the follow-up data, however, is somewhat deflating as the significantly better employment status of the treated patients is the only difference found in the 8 criteria employed, and even this had disappeared a year later (Fairweather and Simon, 1963). No differences were found on any of these criteria: rehospitalization, friendships, interpersonal communication, general adjustment, problem behaviour, degree of illness, alcoholism, or legal violations. At the 18-month follow-up there were no differences whatever between the groups (Fairweather and Simon, 1963). Overall, this study demonstrated the prognostic importance of *diagnosis* in that the short-term psychotic patients tended to do best on most measures. As an attempt to obtain evidence demonstrating the effectiveness of psychotherapy, the study was unsuccessful.

Anker and Walsh (1961) compared the effects of a programme of special activity (drama) with group psychotherapy in 2 matched groups of 28 chronic schizophrenics. Psychotherapy was given in groups of 7, twice a week for $1\frac{1}{2}$ hours per session. The experimental period lasted for a year and the effects of treatment were assessed on a rating scale administered by the nursing staff, who were kept unaware of the group assignments of the patients. The activity programme, devoted largely to drama, produced encouraging results. According to the authors, "the activity variable was responsible for most of the change in behavioural adjustment that occurred", and "it did so with compelling strength and consistency" (p. 480). On the other hand, group psychotherapy produced only one significant result (on motility), and was found to produce non-significant results for all other sub-scores and for the total adjustment score. In terms of trial visits and discharge rates, no differences between the groups were obtained. Although their study encourages the hope that special activity may be of some benefit in the rehabilitation of schizophrenic patients, the inclusion of a routine control group would have strengthened the conclusions reached by Anker and Walsh. While there can be no question about the amount of psychotherapy provided in this study, it can be argued that the psychotherapist who carried out all of the treatment was perhaps ineffective. Be that as it may, Anker and Walsh were unable to produce evidence demonstrating beneficial effects of psychotherapy.

There can be little doubt about the skills of the therapists in the Grinspoon *et al.* (1968) study. They assessed the effects of psychotherapy on 20 chronic schizophrenic patients. All of the patients were given psychotherapy twice weekly for 2 years, but in half of the cases this treatment was supplemented by thioridazine. The remaining 10 patients had their psychotherapy supplemented by placebos. It was found that patients receiving psychotherapy and thioridazine showed some improvement, but there was little sign of change when psychotherapy was combined with placebos. They concluded that "psychotherapy alone (even with experienced psychotherapists) does little or nothing for chronic schizophrenic patients in 2 years; psychotherapy for a much longer period is rarely feasible . . . and its effectiveness therefore becomes a largely academic question" (p. 1651). This useful study would have benefited from an increase in the sample size and the inclusion of a group of patients treated with thioridazine only. On the other hand, one should bear in mind the scale of the effort which the report represents—approximately 200 therapy hours for each of 20 schizophrenic patients. One of the most valuable features of this work is that the treatment was conducted by senior, experienced therapists (mainly psychoanalytic in orientation). It is a curious and regrettable fact that a good deal of our knowledge about the effects of therapy is derived from the efforts of inexperienced therapists.

Turning next to those few studies which have claimed therapeutic successes, Semon and Goldstein (1957) provided group treatment for 32 chronic schizophrenic patients. The effects of 4 slightly varying types of treatment were compared with the changes observed in 7 non-treated control patients. Although they found no differences between the 4 variants of treatment, the authors claimed that they were all superior to the no-treatment conditions. In fact, there were no differences between the treated and untreated patients on total improvement scores or on 2 of the sub-scales which contributed to the total score. There was a slight superiority on the interpersonal sub-scale, however. Nonetheless, the clinical significance of this finding is doubtful as there was a 7-point difference between the treatment and no-treatment groups before psychotherapy commenced. After the completion of psychotherapy, the treated patients were only 5 points better off than the control patients, who had undergone a 2-point decline. The minimal clinical significance of this change is amply shown by the range of pre-treatment scores on this particular sub-scale—11 to 91. The failure of the treatment to produce superior results on 3 of the 4 outcome measures raises serious doubts about the validity of their claim, and matters are complicated even further by their apparent failure to avoid rater contamination as the ratings were not carried out "blind". Sacks and Berger (1954) studied the effects of psychotherapy on 28 chronic schizophrenic patients, who were compared with 28 similar patients admitted at the same time but, for some unspecified reason, not treated. No pretherapy matching on clinical status or diagnosis was ensured. At termination, the treated patients were showing better behaviour on the ward, but there were no differences in discharge rates and no differences on referral to wards for more disturbed patients. In fact, 21% of the patients receiving psychotherapy were sent to disturbed wards. Their poorly chosen control group and their failure to provide comparable general stimulation for both groups casts doubt on the claims made by Sacks and Berger. Ignoring these serious defects, the most that could be said for this study is that psychotherapy may result in improved ward behaviour, but there is no evidence to suggest that it alters the prognosis for this condition. Feifel and Schwartz (1953) claimed to have obtained success in a group of acutely disturbed psychotic patients who received psychotherapy. Unfortunately, their control group was inappropriately selected. Moreover, both the control and experimental group patients were simultaneously receiving other treatments, including physical techniques such as shock therapy, drugs, and even individual psychotherapy. The outcome data are poor, and their follow-up data of little value.

These outcome studies present a bleak picture and appear to confirm only too well the early pessimism expressed by Freud. The better-executed studies yield uniformly negative outcomes, while the favourable claims are based on studies which are manifestly poor—and even then the claims are modest. In spite of all of this unfavourable evidence or, perhaps because of it, the literature on this subject is teeming with conflicting opinions, extravagant assertions, and contradictory recommendations. The literature is best described as chaotic.

Repeatedly one encounters debates and discussions about whether or not the establishment of transference relationships is possible or even desirable, whether the patients should be encouraged or discouraged to regress, whether interpretations should be offered or withheld, and so on. The methods of treatment range from attempts at orthodox psychoanalytic treatment to the deliberate encouragement of infantile behaviour. The more orthodox techniques are sufficiently well known not to require any description, but some of the extraordinary variations are worth mentioning. Although it should be remembered that *these techniques are not widely practised*, they feature in most discussions of psychotherapy in psychotic conditions and are accorded serious consideration and, sometimes, praise. Rosenthal (1962) has described rather well the curiously uncritical attitude adopted by therapists and writers on the subject. He has observed that "the therapists seem to have an unwritten agreement to respect and admire each other's artistry, despite glaring differences and contradictions in points of view, and at the same time to resist concepts and formulations forged in the laboratory, as though the latter were somehow debasing". Two radical variants of psychotherapy will suffice to illustrate the range of practices.

Azima and Wittkower (1956) argue that the frustrated oral and anal needs of "a schizophrenic organism can be gratified by allowing a deep but transitory regression to occur" (p. 122). They describe the treatment of 6 patients over a period of 6 months consisting of 1 hour of treatment 5 days a week. The main feature of their treatment was "offering the patients primitive media", as it was their purpose to "provide a symbolic miniature infantile situation, in which appropriate feelings could be expressed". The treatment was divided into 3 phases with the first consisting of an emphasis on anal needs. "The media offered were mud, brown clay, cocoa powder, cocoa mud, plasticine, and finger paint. In addition, aggressive activities such as tearing paper and throwing darts were introduced. Patients were encouraged to smear and soil, and to cut and throw objects" (p. 122). During the second phase they concentrated on oral gratifications, and additional aggressive activities were introduced. "Patients were offered a baby bottle filled with milk with large holes in the nipple; at first they were also fed with liquids 15 minutes before the end of each session" (p. 123). In the third phase, more structured activities were introduced: "jumping ropes, playing with dolls, listening to music and dancing, working with clay and making pots, drawing on the blackboard and cleaning it, playing games such as badminton and ping-pong, and colouring children's books" (p. 123).

Rosen (1953) developed a variation on psychoanalysis which he calls "direct analysis" and for which he claims considerable therapeutic value. He reports cures following a course of treatment which may last from 3 days to 11 months, with the average period of treatment lasting from 2 to 3 months. In attempting to achieve his goal of a complete analysis of the transference "as we aim to do in ordinary analytic procedures", he adopted some extremely radical procedures. According to Rosen (p. 8), "the governing principle of direct analysis is that the therapist must be a loving, omnipotent protector and provider for the patient. Expressed another way, he must be the idealized mother who now has the responsibility of bringing the patient up all over again . . . since direct analysis holds that this catastrophic collapse is the consequence of unconscious malevolent mothering" (p. 9). The purpose of the direct interpretations is to indicate to the patient "that somewhere in his environment there now exists understanding, that is, magical, omnipotent understanding, the earliest understanding of him exhibited by an adult in his neonatal environment" (p. 12). In the first place the therapist has to provide for the "conscious, tangible needs of the patient which anyone can recognize, such as food, warmth, and protection". He then employs a variety of techniques designed to provide the patient with insight into his unconscious and, thereby, a resolution of the psychosis. Having achieved this goal, it is desirable to complete treatment with a course of orthodox psychoanalysis.

The techniques which Rosen employs are described in his own book and, rather more systematically, by Scheflen (1961), who spent 2 years observing and recording Rosen's treatment of several psychotic patients at the Temple University Medical Center. Scheflen lists 16 techniques: promising and rewarding, threatening and punishing, suggesting and instructing, coercing, rendering service, group pressure, ridiculing and discrediting, interrupting and diverting, appealing and challenging, offering alternatives, misrepresenting, imitating, role-playing, acting out, reassuring, and confrontation and interpretation. According to Scheflen, whose account is detached and occasionally favourable, the "principal techniques of direct analysis" are discrediting, arousal of shame, and ridiculing. In order to achieve certain therapeutic aims, Rosen attempts to weaken the patients' relationships with other people. For example, a female patient was isolated from her relatives because she "resisted relating" to the therapist. "A woman patient persistently refused to recognize any relatedness to Rosen, insisting on talking about her husband or one of the assistants. Rosen took various measures to break her attachment to the husband. He finally told her that her husband had divorced her and remarried. Multiple 'proofs' of this were conjured, and it was weeks before the patient was told that this was not so" (p. 125). In another case, Rosen was attempting to improve the patient's sexual adjustment. The description given by Scheflen is as follows: "with this patient, months were spent on this matter. Rosen insisted that the patient have intercourse with him. He interpreted her flight from this idea as a fear of incest and he intermittently reassured her that there would never be a sexual relationship between them. At first these reassurances were nearly always followed by a temporary remission of many of the patient's psychotic symptoms. Later Rosen omitted the reassurances . . . in the sequence to be related, Rosen spent about 20 minutes forcing the patient by coercion and threats to state that now she sexually preferred Rosen to her husband but would later prefer her husband. She resisted in all manners but finally said what she was told" (p. 159). The extract concludes with this exchange:

"ROSEN: I am going to get you, I'll make you kiss the black on the floor. (*Rosen approached patient menacingly and forced her to her knees.*)
PATIENT: Oh, no, don't.
ROSEN: Say you prefer me . . . say it" (p. 160).

In a subsequent session with the same patient, she asked Rosen if she should take her skirt down. He replied affirmatively. "She appeared exhausted, docile. She asked Rosen to help her pull her skirt down. He reached over and pulled them down for her. She put her head on his shoulder and made no further strong defiance. Rosen sent for a blanket, covered her up and began urging her to go to sleep. As the patient complied, acting sleepy, passive and child-like, Rosen reversed his field and twice provoked a repetition of the cycle" (p. 173). Other examples of the therapist's behaviour can be conveyed in a selection of Scheflen's quotations from Rosen. "Your mother killed your sister" (a reference to a sibling who was scalded to death by falling into a tub while the mother was washing) (p. 128). "I am God and will not permit you to be harmed" (p. 95). "The milk is warm and good. Not the poison that your mother fed you" (Rosen, 1953, p. 21).

Presumably this type of conduct is defensible. It cannot be said, however, that an explanation readily springs to mind. It will come as no surprise that the therapeutic value of this technique has never been demonstrated despite Rosen's claims. Scheflen (1961) adopted a reserved position on the patients he had seen treated, but Horwitz *et al.* (1958) followed up 19 of Rosen's original 37 cases and concluded, "whatever the merits of direct analytic therapy for schizophrenia, the claim that it results in a high degree of recovery remains unproven" (p. 783).

Perhaps the last word on this dismal scene should rest with Rosenthal. Recalling the satirical statement that psychotherapy is "an undefined technique applied to unspecified problems with unpredictable outcomes. For this technique we recommend rigorous training", he then records his astonishment at finding the following statement in a book on psychotherapy with schizophrenics, published in 1961. He assures us that the statement is intended to be taken seriously: "there is no general agreement as to what constitutes necessary, specific personal or professional attributes for the successful therapist with schizophrenic patients, except that to be a successful therapist with schizophrenic patients demands extensive training and desirable personal qualities".

CHAPTER 10

THE DEVELOPMENT
OF BEHAVIOURAL THERAPY

IN HIS opening address delivered to the Nineteenth International Congress of Psychology in London in 1969, the then Secretary of State for Social Services, Mr. Richard Crossman, acknowledged the public arrival of advances in behavioural methods:

"The third example I will give of a real, genuine scientific breakthrough is behaviour therapy. I would only add that this is something which I didn't previously know much about, but which has impressed me since I have been Minister, as something which will be of very great beneficial value when it has been adequately developed." This discussion considers the progress achieved so far.

Some of the pioneers of behaviour therapy were solely concerned with the practical applications of experimental psychology and, particularly, with the implications of what was known as learning theory; others viewed their efforts as a deliberate attempt to develop an effective substitute for psychotherapy. The rapid and extensive growth of behaviour therapy during the past decade has turned that aim into a tawdry ambition. It appears likely that behaviour therapy will prove to be a successful step in the development of a scientifically based approach to treatment by psychological means. Its range of application already exceeds that of psychotherapy, and even includes chronically ill psychotic patients and intellectually retarded children and adults.

The danger of a premature and uncritical celebration of this advance in clinical psychology appears to have passed, and sober assessments of the progress achieved to date have been undertaken (e.g. Franks, 1969; Marks, 1969; Bandura, 1969). Less abstemious accounts have also been given by Rachman (1968) and by Rachman and Teasdale (1969). The general opinion of most writers on the subject, expressed with varying degrees of confidence, is that the behavioural techniques are capable of producing significant clinical improvements in certain types of patient. The disagreements among writers tend to centre on the extent to which supplementary treatment is desirable, the range of effectiveness of the techniques and perhaps, most important of all, the mechanisms involved in therapeutic change.

Nevertheless, some important and generally accepted advances have been made. The introduction of behaviour therapy provoked numerous objections particularly among psychodynamic writers. Two of the most serious and widely expressed criticisms were these. Firstly, it was argued that the direct treatment of manifest neurotic behaviour would, if successful, lead to "symptom substitution". That is to say the patient would develop new and possibly worse symptoms if the so-called defensive reactions were removed. The phenomenon of symptom substitution has, in the event, proved to be of minimal importance and occurs rarely. In none of the numerous experiments mentioned below was symptom substitution observed to be a problem even though in many studies it was the subject of careful scrutiny. In the clinical reports on behaviour therapy the occurrence of symptom substitution is also a rarity (Rachman, 1968).

A second objection was based on the claim that it is impossible to bring about the reduction or elimination of neurotic "symptoms" or behaviour unless one first eliminates the putative basic cause of the disorder. It was argued that behaviour therapy could not succeed because the therapist's attention was incorrectly directed. This objection has now been excluded. The experimental investigations and clinical reports have produced evidence that substantial improvements in abnormal behaviour can be obtained by systematic desensitization and other methods of behaviour therapy even when little or no attention is paid to the putative underlying causes of the illness.

No convincing psychodynamic explanation of the effects of behavioural therapy has yet appeared. As far as psychodynamic theory is concerned, behaviour therapy remains inexplicable.

The existence of several reviews of recent vintage makes it unnecessary to describe in detail the present status of the experimental and clinical evidence on the subject of behaviour therapy. For present purposes, a summary of the evidence will serve. The present account is supplemented by a description of the drift of current thinking and an indication of some outstanding problems.

Systematic desensitization is a technique developed by Wolpe for the treatment of neurotic disorders in which anxiety is a central element. It has been used extensively in the treatment of neurotic patients (Wolpe, 1958; Rachman, 1968; Marks, 1969), and the procedure and its rationale have been the subject of numerous experimental investigations (Rachman, 1967). The technique involves the gradual and graduated imaginal presentation of anxiety-evoking scenes while the patient is deeply relaxed. The patient acquires the ability to tolerate the anxiety-evoking stimuli in his imagination, and this improvement usually transfers to the real situation. Much of our knowledge about phobias has been obtained from the study of normal subjects who show an excessive fear of spiders, snakes, worms, and the like.* In 1963 Lang and Lazovik reported the results of an experiment carried out on non-psychiatric subjects who suffered from an excessive fear of snakes. This pioneer experiment was carefully prepared and executed and has provided a model for some 40 subsequent studies. The authors found that their experimental analogue of Wolpe's desensitization therapy effectively reduced snake-phobic behaviour. Their subjects showed subjective and overt reductions of fear, and these improvements were maintained at the 6-month follow-up period. In a subsequent experiment Lang and his colleagues (1966) demonstrated beyond question that the desensitization technique produces a specific therapeutic change over and above any modifications of a non-specific nature which might arise from the therapeutic preliminaries or atmosphere. Subjects who were given a cleverly designed form of pseudo-therapy showed little change. It was also found to be unnecessary for the therapists to delve into the presumed basic causes of their subjects' fear of snakes. They also found that the development of a therapeutic relationship with the therapist was not sufficient to bring about changes in the phobia. Their results also

* This information about fear of insects and animals has not yet had any influence on psychodynamic theories. For example, Newman and Stoller (1969) in their account on a recent case claim that the psychoanalysis of their patient confirmed Abraham's old view that the spider symbolizes bisexual genitalia. If so, "fear of bisexual genitalia" is readily desensitized in a few sessions.

encouraged the belief that desensitization of a specific fear generalizes in a positive fashion to other fears and that all-round improvements might be expected.

Virtually all of the conclusions reached by Lang and his colleagues have been confirmed by other experimenters. The extent of these investigations can be gauged from the summary tables (Table 4). I know of no other psychotherapeutic undertaking which has yielded such widespread agreement.

These studies, in addition to the support which they provide for Wolpe's work and Lang's experiments, have also explored the nature of the desensitization process in detail. For example, attempts have been made to isolate the effective elements in the treatment. Thus far the evidence suggests that desensitization effects are potentiated by the combined action of relaxation instructions and graduated image presentations (Rachman, 1965; Davison, 1968; Kondas, 1967; Lomont and Edwards, 1967). However, the role and action of muscle relaxation training, as originally stated, has been the subject of critical re-examination (Rachman, 1968; Nawas et al., 1970).

The present state of the experimental evidence on desensitization permits the following conclusions. Desensitization therapy effectively reduces phobic behaviour. It is unnecessary to ascertain the origin of the phobia in order to eliminate it and neither is it necessary to change the subject's basic attitudes or to modify his personality. The elimination of a phobia is rarely followed by symptom substitution. The response to treatment is not related to the trait of suggestibility. Relaxation alone, or accompanied by pseudo-therapeutic interviews, does not reduce phobias. The establishment of a therapeutic relationship with the patient does not of itself reduce the phobia. Interpretive therapy combined with relaxation does not reduce phobic behaviour. The induction of a state of subjective relaxation facilitates desensitization but is not a prerequisite. The technique can be used effectively even when the subject is not in a state of muscular relaxation. Although imaginal presentations of the fear-evoking stimuli confer numerous practical advantages and increased therapeutic flexibility, there is sufficient evidence to show that real-life exposures can be effective, particularly if they are carried out in a graduated manner (e.g. Goldstein, 1969; Garfield et al., 1967; Bandura, 1969). In certain circumstances, real-life exposures

TABLE 4

THE EFFECTS OF DESENSITIZATION (ANALOGUE STUDIES)

Authors	Type of anxiety	Desensitization			Type of control	Sample	Assessment			Outcome Desens. more effective?
		Individual	Group	Other			Subj.	Behav.	Psycho-metric	
Lang and Lazovik (1963)	Snake phobia	Yes	—	—	No-treatment after prelimiary training	E = 13, C = 11	Yes	Yes	Yes	On all 3 measures
Lang et al. (1966)	Snake phobia	Yes	—	—	Pseudo-therapy	E = 10, C = 10	Yes	Yes	Yes	On all 3 measures
Rachman (1965)	Spider phobic	—	Yes	—	Relaxation only or Desensitization only or no treatment	n = 12	Yes	Yes	Yes	On subjective and behaviour measures
Davison (1968)	Snake phobic	Yes	—	—	Relaxation only or desensitization only or no treatment	n = 28	Yes	Yes	Yes	On all measures
Paul (1966)	Public speaking	Yes	—	—	Insight, attention, no treatment	n = 60	Yes	Yes	Yes	On all measures
Paul and Shannon (1966)	Public speaking	—	Yes	—	No treatment	n = 20	Yes	Yes	Yes	On all measures
Kondas (1967)	Examinations	—	Yes	—	Relaxation, no treatment, hierarchy only	n = 36	Yes	—	Yes	On all measures
Lazarus (1961)	Acrophobia, etc.	—	Yes	—	Relaxation and insight	n = 35	Yes	—	Yes	Both measures
Cooke (1966) Rats	Rats	Yes	—	In vivo	No treatment	n = 12	Yes	Yes	—	Both measures
Lomont and Edwards (1967)	Snake phobic	Yes	—	—	Without relaxation	n = 22	Yes	Yes	Yes	On 3 of 5 measures
Johnson and Sechrest (1968)	Test anxiety	—	Yes	—	Relaxation, no treatment	n = 33	Yes	Yes	Yes	Only on achievement tests
Ramsay et al. (1966)	Animals	Yes	—	—	Massed practice	n = 20	Yes	Yes	—	Yes, when spaced
Moore (1965)	Asthma attacks	Yes	—	—	Within subject, relaxation only Vs. in vivo	n = 12	Yes	Yes	—	On peak flow measure
Garfield et al. (1967)	Snake phobia	—	Yes	In vivo	in vivo but inadequate	n = 7	Yes	Yes	—	In vivo adds something?
Katahn et al. (1966)	Examinations	—	Yes	Plus counselling	No treatment	n = 28	Yes	—	Yes	Yes?

TABLE 4 (cont.)

Authors	Type of anxiety	Desensitization			Type of control	Sample	Assessment			Outcome Desens. more effective?
		Individual	Group	Other			Subj.	Behav.	Psychometric	
Emery and Krumbolz (1967)	Examinations	Yes	—	Plus standard hierarchy	No treatment	$n = 36$	Yes	Yes	Yes	On subjective and psychometric
Garlington and Cotler (1968)	Examination	—	Yes	—	No treatment	$n = 32$	Yes	Yes	Yes	On subjective and psycho-metric
Suinn (1968)	Examinations	Yes	Yes	—	No treatment	$n = 32$	Yes	—	Yes	On subjective and psycho-metric
Zeisset (1968)	Interviews	Yes	—	—	No treatment, relax, attention	$n = 48$ psychotics	Yes	Yes	—	On both measures
Donner and Guerney (1969)	Examinations	—	Yes	Auto-mated	No treatment, therapist absent	$n = 42$	Yes	Yes	Yes	On all measures
Lanyon et al. (1968)	Spider phobic	Yes	—	Massed	Massed, pseudo-treatment	$n = 17$	Yes	Yes	Yes	Trend on all measures
Melamed and Lang (1967)	Snake phobia	Yes	—	Auto-mated	Automation, no treatment	$n = 21$	Yes	Yes	Yes	On all measures
Kahn and Baker (1968)	Mixed phobias	Yes	—	Self-treatment	Self-treatment	$n = 16$	Yes	—	—	Self-treatment equally effective?
Cohen (1969)	Test anxiety	—	Yes	—	No treatment	$E = 13$, $C = 8$	Yes	Yes	Yes	On all measures
Oliveau et al. (1969)	Snake phobia	—	Yes	—	Praise/instructions (?)	$n = 32$	Yes	Yes	—	Yes; importance of instructions
Cotler and Garlington (1969)	Snake phobia	Yes	—	—	No treatment	$E = 12$, 7; $C = 7$	—	Yes	Yes	Yes, all measures
Crighton and Jehu (1969)	Test anxiety	—	Yes	—	Psychotherapy	$E = 10$, $C = 7$	Yes	Yes	Yes	No
O'Neill and Howell (1969)	Snake phobia	—	Yes	—	(a) In vivo (b) Slides	$E = 10$, $C^1 = 10$, $C^2 = 10$	—	Yes	—	All groups improved
Robinson and Suinn (1969)	Spiders	Yes	Yes	—	Group vs. individual	$E = 10$, $C = 10$	—	Yes	Yes	All measures; massing effective
Mann and Rosenthal (1969)	Test anxiety	—	Yes	Vicarious	No treatment	$E^1 = 25$, $E^2 = 25$,	Yes	Yes	Yes	On all 6 measures

TABLE 4 (contd.)

Authors	Type of anxiety	Desensitization			Type of control	Sample	Assessment			Outcome Desens. more effective?
		Individual	Group	Other			Subj.	Behav.	Psychometric	
Willis and Edwards (1969)	Mice	—	Yes	Implosion	No treatment	$C = 21$, $E^1 = 16$, $E^2 = 16$	Yes	Yes	Yes	On all 6 measures
Crowder and Thornton (1970)	Snake phobic	Yes	—	—	No treatment	$C = 16$, $E^1 = 10$, $E^2 = 10$, $C = 9$	—	Yes	Yes	Yes, but muscle relaxation redundant
Nawas et al. (1970)	Snake phobic	—	Yes	—	Pseudo-treatment, no treatment	$E^1 = 10$, $E^2 = 10$, $C^1 = 10$	—	Yes	—	Yes
Miller and Nawas (1970)	Snake phobic	—	Yes	—	Pseudo-treatment, no treatment	$E^1 = 10$, $E^2 = 10$, $C^1 = 10$	Yes	Yes	—	Yes
Nawas et al. (1970)	Snake phobic	—	Yes	—	Pseudo-treatment, no treatment	$E^1 = 10$, $E^2 = 10$, $E^3 = 10$, $C^1 = 10$	—	Yes	—	Yes, but muscle relaxation redundant
Mitchell and Ingham (1970)	Test anxiety	—	Yes	—	No treatment, no contact	$E = 31$, $C^1 = 6$, $C^2 = 22$	—	Yes	Yes	Yes
McGlynn and Mapp (1970)	Snake	—	Yes	—	No treatment	$E^1 = 8$, $E^2 = 8$, $E^3 = 8$	—	Yes	—	Yes
Proctor (1969)	Snake	—	Yes (?)	—	No treatment	$C = 7$, $E = 54$	Yes	3	—	Yes on 3 out of 4 measures
Cotler (1970)	Snake	—	Yes	Automated	No treatment	$C = 9$, $E^1 = 16$	Yes	Yes	Yes	Yes, all measures
Barrett (1969)	Snake	Yes	—	—	(i) No treatment (ii) Implosion	$C = 12$, $n = 36$	Yes	Yes	Yes	Both more effective than control; implosion quicker but less stable

are more effective. There is evidence that desensitization can be carried out as an automated procedure (Melamed and Lang, 1967; Donner and Guerney, 1969; Kahn and Baker, 1968). Although the practical consequences of automated or self-administered desensitization (Kahn and Baker, 1968) should not be underestimated, their theoretical significance is more important. Without necessarily discounting the possible contribution which the therapist's presence might make, it is clear that a wholly satisfactory explanation of desensitization effects must take into account the expendability of the therapist. Certainly, any theoretical account which depends entirely or largely on the personality or even on the presence of the therapist is unlikely to succeed. It follows also that explanations which are couched solely in terms of the relationship which is established between the subject and his therapist cannot be successful. It can, of course, be argued that some type of relationship is established even through the medium of a subject-operated tape-recorder. Recourse to some form of "disembodied" relationship theory will of course have to forfeit its theoretical antecedents and is unlikely to attract enthusiastic support.

In addition to the evidence derived directly from research on desensitization, two other techniques for reducing fear (both developed within the last 5 years) must enter into any consideration of the nature and mode of action of desensitization. Although the rationale proposed by Stampfl and his colleagues (e.g. Stampfl, 1967; Hogan, 1968) to account for the effects of implosive therapy is unconvincing, the investigations which arise from such a consideration are of great interest. Despite its theoretical weaknesses (Rachman, 1969), the results of the implosive method reported by Hogan and his co-workers are remarkable in claiming substantial reductions of fear after exceptionally brief treatment periods. Their claims are particularly interesting because they are concordant with numerous experimental findings in the animal literature (Rachman, 1969) and because of the encouraging clinical findings recently obtained by Marks and his colleagues (e.g. Boulougouris et al., 1971). Another procedure which has yielded exceptionally good experimental results is modelling—a subject which Bandura (1969) and his colleagues have revivified over the past few years. The modelling technique deserves an honourable mention if for no other reason than the fact that it was the first experimental technique to produce demonstrably better results than desensitization in at least 1 study.

A direct link between desensitization, implosion, and modelling can be found in the common emphasis on the absence or elimination of primary aversive reinforcement. Since the non-occurrence of anticipated aversive consequences is a prerequisite for the extinction of fear, it is argued that the modelling displays which are most likely to have strong effects on phobic observers are those in which the performances that the observers regard as hazardous are repeatedly shown to be safe under a variety of threatening circumstances—and preferably by different models. In regard to the characteristic which so clearly distinguishes desensitization from implosion—graduated approximation—Bandura argued that while such graduation is not a necessary condition for vicarious extinction, it nevertheless permits greater control over the process. In brief, some of the major therapeutic findings to have emerged so far from the work of Bandura (1969) and his colleagues are as follows. Symbolic modelling "is less powerful than live demonstrations" of the same behaviour (Bandura and Menlove, 1968). Real-life modelling is a powerful treatment and can be further augmented by combining it with guided participation (Bandura and Menlove, 1968). This finding has been supported in a subsequent study of Ritter's (1968) on snake-phobic children.

The ideas and technology of operant conditioning have so far proved to be less successful in the treatment of neurotic behaviour than they have been in generating adaptive behaviour in severely handicapped patients (see page 156). The limited amount of research on the subject (Wagner and Cauthen, 1968; Oliveau, 1969) suggests that useful reductions in phobic behaviour can be obtained by manipulating the social reinforcement consequent on behavioural changes. These findings, although limited in scope, are unsurprising and reassuring, for it would be disconcerting if phobic behaviour were found to be entirely unresponsive to this type of reinforcement. Nevertheless, it appears improbable that a satisfactory explanation of desensitization and other fear-reducing techniques can be managed exclusively within operant conditioning terms. Apart from other problems, an operant explanation based on social reinforcement would have difficulty in accounting for the effect of automated treatment and self-administered treatment.

Before examining the clinical effectiveness of desensitization and related procedures, a short digression is necessary. There have been numerous attempts to account for the experimental evidence summarized above, but for the present we will be concerned only with the most prominent of these. Wolpe's (1958) own explanation for the effects of desensitization and related types of treatment is based on the concept of reciprocal inhibition, and he argues that the therapeutic benefit of the technique derives from the repeated inhibition of unadaptive anxiety. The greatest part of the accumulated evidence is consistent with Wolpe's theory, and some additional support has been produced recently by Donner and by Grings. The experiment of Donner and Guerney (1969) showed that the fearful subjects who showed the greatest improvement after treatment were those who relaxed well and who obtained clear and evocative images on instruction. Along different lines, but equally encouraging, is the experiment by Grings and Uno (1968), who obtained experimental evidence in support of the claim that relaxation can reciprocally inhibit fear responses. Wolpe's theory is not without its difficulties, however. It has been observed that at crucial points the theory is not sufficiently explicit, that the attempt to draw an analogy between a physiological process of inhibition and a psychological one is unsatisfactory, that fear and relaxation are not necessarily antagonistic, and so on. On the practical side, it now seems probable that desensitization can occur even in the absence of muscle relaxation or, indeed, any deliberately imposed antagonistic response. Other evidence which is a little more difficult to account for with Wolpe's theory includes the recent work on implosion and on modelling. The implosive technique, far from involving a process of reciprocal inhibition, consists of the prolonged elicitation of a strong emotional reaction. In fact, some time ago Wolpe himself raised the possibility of developing treatment techniques based on reactive inhibition as well as reciprocal inhibition. The fact remains, however, that the recent results obtained by the implosive method cannot be accommodated within Wolpe's reciprocal inhibition model, and while this need not affect the validity of the theory, it does mean that processes other than reciprocal inhibition can be and sometimes are involved in the reduction of fear. The effectiveness of modelling can be encompassed within Wolpe's model by making the assumption that observing a fearless model interact with the fearful stimuli in some way succeeds in inducing a state which is antagonistic to fear. This assumption, although it is not intrinsically unreasonable, will be difficult to confirm. At this stage it certainly seems easier to view modelling as an example of an extinction process rather than one of inhibition. Gellhorn's (1964) theory of a hypothalamic balance resembles Wolpe's theory at a molecular level. Although Gellhorn's scheme is in many ways appealing, it appears to be insufficient to account for the effects of desensitization therapy. It encounters two difficulties: in the first place the current evidence suggests that relaxation by itself is not the mechanism which produces therapeutic improvements and, secondly, his model is useful in attempting to understand the mode of anxiety suppression, but it seems unable to explain the reason for the permanent reduction of anxiety reactions.

In an interesting and provocative alternative, Lader and Wing (1966) suggested that desensitization could be "more simply regarded as straightforward habituation carried out when the habituation rate is maximal, i.e. with the patient at as low a level of activity as possible". On the basis of their own and related evidence they suggested that this habituation process is facilitated in treatment by relaxing the patient. While in this state of low activity, he is then subjected to repeated minimal stimulation, thereby ensuring that habituation will take place efficiently. This model has now been elaborated by Lader and Mathews (1968), who made proposals about the onset and course of phobic conditions based on the habituation model. One of the appealing features of the hypothesis is that it enables one to examine a series of testable predictions. The details of the hypothesis, the ensuing predictions, and their current status are discussed in detail in Rachman (1969). Some of the difficulties encountered by the habituation model are as follows. The durability of habituation effects remains an open question. Secondly, the model has some difficulty in accounting for the persistence of monosymptomatic phobias: in terms of the Lader hypothesis these patients should have a low arousal level and rapid habituation. Consequently it is difficult to see why naturally occurring habituation does not wipe out these often long-standing fears. Thirdly, and perhaps most important of all, it seems unlikely that the habituation model would have been able to predict the successful results of the flooding technique (Rachman, 1969).

It has been shown experimentally that fear can be reduced by desensitization or by the flooding technique or by modelling. We also know from both clinical and experimental studies that a proportion of people overcome their excessive fears without having received specific treatment (see Chapter 3 and Rachman, 1968). These combined findings pose a problem. Is there a single process common to all these phenomena?

Wolpe's theory of reciprocal inhibition is still able to accommodate the available evidence on desensitization, and it may even be possible to extend it to encompass modelling treatments. It seems unlikely, however, to account for the effects of flooding techniques. If the reciprocal inhibition model cannot subsume all of the procedures, does the alternative theory put forward by Lader, Wing, and Mathews supply this need?

Lader and Wing (1966) and Lader and Mathews (1968) have made explicit attempts to account for the effects of desensitization within their habituation scheme, and the modelling technique can also be regarded as a process of graded habituation. Bandura (1969) and his colleagues have convincingly demonstrated that extinction of fear can occur vicariously, and Bandura himself came close to stating the habituation position: "repeated modelling of approach responses decreases the arousal potential aversive stimuli below the threshold for activating avoidance responses" (Bandura, 1969). Extrapolating from the habituation model, one could predict that modelling treatment will proceed more rapidly and effectively if the patient's level of arousal is reduced early in the treatment session. The habituation model can also accommodate another result obtained by Bandura and Menlove (1968), who found that exposure to multiple fearless models produced more extensive improvements. Similarly, the findings that real models are more effective than symbolic models and that the addition of live participation both aid therapeutic recovery are consistent with the habituation model. The habituation model strikes real difficulty, however, in attempting to account for the effects of flooding treatments. Although some explanations for overcoming this obstacle have been suggested (e.g. Rachman, 1969), they tend to circumvent the problem rather than absorb it.

As will be evident from this brief résumé, it is becoming increasingly difficult to maintain a unitary theory to account for the reduction of anxiety by behavioural techniques. It is too early to admit defeat, but the likelihood of complementary hypotheses being required seems to increase with the rapid accumulation of new evidence.

Clinical Results

The clinical effectiveness of behaviour therapy (and desensitization in particular) is attested to by two types of evidence: individual case histories (of didactic value only) and field trials. A large number of illustrative case histories are now available, and many of them have been conveniently assembled and reproduced in 3 or 4 texts. Descriptions of the clinical method are contained in: *Behaviour Therapy and the Neuroses*, edited by H. J. Eysenck; *The Causes and Cures of Neuroses* by Eysenck and Rachman; *Psychotherapy by Reciprocal Inhibition* by Wolpe; *Case Studies in Behaviour Modification* by Ullmann and Krasner; *Fears and Phobias* by Marks; *The Practice of Behaviour Therapy* by Wolpe.

The first major report on the clinical effectiveness of desensitization and related methods was provided by Wolpe in 1958. He described the results obtained in the treatment of 210 neurotic patients. Wolpe accepted every patient referred provided that the diagnosis of neurosis had been confirmed. The composition of the sample is adequately described, and it is clear that the majority of his patients were suffering from anxiety states of one type or another. They were not subdivided into phobics and related conditions, so that it is not possible to provide an accurate estimate of the degree of success which was obtained with specifically phobic disorders. However, 135 of the 210 patients reported in this publication were described as being anxiety neurotics; an examination of the case descriptions suggests that many of them were complaining of phobic symptoms of one variety or another.

Wolpe assessed the effectiveness of therapy in terms of Knight's 5 criteria (see p. 45): symptomatic improvement, increased productiveness, improved adjustment and pleasure in sex, improved interpersonal relationships, and the ability to deal with reasonable reality stresses. Each patient was classified in terms of these criteria into 1 of 5 categories: apparently cured, much improved, moderately improved, slightly improved, and unimproved. Of the 210 patients treated, approximately 90% were apparently cured or much improved after treatment.

This exceptionally successful result must be regarded with a measure of reserve because of the incomplete nature of the follow-up investigations. It was impossible, for practical reasons, to arrange long-term follow-ups for the majority of these patients, and it seems probable, in view of more recent evidence, that a proportion of them did not maintain their initial improvements. Other possible sources of inflation in this figure are rater contamination and Wolpe's exclusion from the final assessment of those patients who had not completed a minimum of 15 treatment sessions. This is an unusually stringent criterion and one which most non-analytic clinicians have not used.

This report by Wolpe was the first major account of the systematic attempt to apply principles of learning theory to the treatment of neurotic disturbances. As a pioneering effort it cannot, of course, be expected to provide a full answer to the problems of therapy. It is, nevertheless, true (and this can be said with increasing confidence in light of recent evidence) that the therapy and general approach developed by Wolpe constitutes an advance in our ability to treat neurotic disturbances and phobias in particular.

Wolpe's work is attractive for a number of reasons in addition to the encouraging therapeutic outcome which he obtained. It was developed in a systematic and logical manner from existing theoretical notions and specially devised experiments. It has the further advantage of being stated and described in a manner which permits or even attracts experimental investigation of both the assumptions and actual procedures involved.

In 1963 Lazarus reported on the treatment of 408 neurotic patients. They were treated on the lines described by Wolpe and were assessed in similar manner. Lazarus was able to obtain significant improvement in 321 of his patients, that is, 78%. He then went on to carry out a detailed analysis of the results obtained with 126 patients who were suffering from what he describes as "severe neurosis". This sub-analysis was carried out in an attempt to estimate the effectiveness of behaviour therapy with more complex and severe disorders. Lazarus found that the recovery rate in severe cases was only 62%. This figure is, of course, lower than that obtained in the total series and also lower than that obtained by Wolpe in his major report. This sub-analysis suggests that while behaviour therapy is probably effective in treating complex neurotic disorders, it may be more effective in treating simple disorders. Another difference which might account for the reduced improvement rate in Lazarus's group is the fact that each of the 126 severely neurotic patients was followed up for a mean duration of 2 years. It will also be noticed that this figure is close to the crude spontaneous remission rate for undifferentiated neurotic cases. The absence of controls and the likelihood of rater contamination are additional reasons for treating the results with reserve.

Other clinical reports have been provided by Hussain (1964), Burnett and Ryan (1963), and Schmidt et al. (1965). As these 3 clinical reports all described variations on conventional behaviour therapy, and because they dealt with a mixture of different types of patient, they will not be discussed in any detail here. It is sufficient to say that the success rates varied between 60% and 95% and that the suggestion emerged from the paper by Schmidt et al. that patients who had chronic and complicated disorders tended on the whole to do less well than those patients who were less severely ill.

Humphery (1966) reported a comparison trial between behaviour therapy and psychotherapy in treating neurotic disorders in children. Both methods produced successful results, but behaviour therapy was slightly more effective and was significantly quicker than psycho-therapy. The long-term results from behaviour therapy were found to be superior. The value of this trial is limited by inadequate agreement between the independent "blind" assessors and by a slight overlap in the 2 methods of therapy, both of which were carried out by the same therapist.

Some years ago, Cooper (1963) reported a retrospective study of the effects of behaviour therapy. He carried out a follow-up study of 30 patients who had received various types of exploratory behaviour therapy at the Maudsley Hospital between 1954 and 1960. Cooper attempted to construct a retrospective control group by matching the key patients with another 30 who had been treated by other methods at approximately the same time. In fact, he was able to obtain only 16 matched controls from the hospital records. The progress of these matched pairs of patients (10 phobics, 4 obsessional, 1 stammerer, and 1 case of writer's cramp) was estimated by 2 independent assessors. Retrospective assessments were made of their progress at the end of treatment and 1 month and 1 year after treatment. Cooper stated that the "only striking finding is at the end of treatment for the 10 phobic patients, 9 of whom showed definite improvement in the symptom treatment compared to only 5 of the control cases". The superior improvement observed in the phobic patients was not apparent at the follow-up assessment. Cooper also pointed out that none of the patients had developed substitute symptoms.

Unfortunately, the value of Cooper's study is undermined by several factors. The selection of patients was not properly randomized as the matching was carried out retrospectively, and, as Cooper himself points out, "in some of these cases, behaviour therapy suffered the fate of all new forms of treatment and was tried as a last resort, and some cases were taken on as much experimentally as therapeutically. This was particularly so in obsessional patients. . . ."

Some of the treatment was carried out by students or by psychologists who had no previous experience of behaviour therapy (many of the control patients were treated by trainee psychiatrists). Thirdly, Cooper provides few details about the nature of the behaviour therapy used. His statement that the phobic patients were treated by Wolpe's methods of reciprocal inhibition and desensitization is misleading. In fact, fewer of the patients in the matched group of therapy cases were treated by the method which Wolpe uses in practically all his phobic cases, namely desensitization based on relaxation. Consequently, Cooper's comparison of the results with those reported by Wolpe appears to be unjustified.

Cooper failed to indicate in a clear manner that he was in fact comparing different types of behaviour therapy. Moreover, he was comparing different types of patient—many of the Maudsley group were people who required in-patient hospital care. The great majority of Wolpe's patients were treated on an out-patient basis. A further drawback to Cooper's study was the fact that the assessors worked solely from the case notes and did not interview any of the patients in either the treatment or the control groups. Cooper himself interviewed 14 of the 30 behaviour therapy patients and none of the controls. For these reasons Cooper's conclusions cannot be accepted at face value.

In an extension of Cooper's study, Cooper *et al.* (1965) arrived at a similar conclusion when they examined an additional 37 patients treated at the Maudsley Hospital. They claimed that in none of the treatment groups was behaviour therapy less effective than other methods of treatment and that in the phobias it was more effective. The development of fresh symptoms after successful behaviour treatment was not a hazard. Behaviour therapy can be effective in severe chronic cases where other methods have been tried and failed, and in some conditions (i.e. monosymptomatic phobias) it may even be the first consideration for treatment. The finding that severe chronic patients do not respond as successfully to behaviour therapy as do other types of neurotic patient has now received support in a prospective study.

Marks and Gelder (1966a) described a control trial of behaviour therapy with 20 severe agoraphobic patients. These patients were carefully matched and placed into either the treatment or control group. The therapy consisted of graded retraining in real-life situations together with Wolpe's technique of desensitization in imagination. The control treatment was based on brief "re-educative psychotherapy", and both types of treatment were given 3 times weekly.

In each group 7 out of the 10 patients improved symptomatically. In both instances, however, the patients were left with much residual disability. This disappointing result appears to be attributable to the fact that the patients concerned were severely ill. The mean duration of the agoraphobic illness was more than 7 years, and all the patients were deemed to require in-patient care. As has already been noted in other studies, severely ill patients do not respond as well to behaviour therapy as those with less incapacitating disorders.

Closer inspection of the results indicate, however, that the patients who were treated by behaviour therapy had improved slightly more (but not statistically so) than the other group. Moreover, the behaviour therapy group showed "greater improvement in work capacity . . . at the end of treatment". A similar finding was reported by Hain *et al.* (1966).

The argument that the relatively poor results obtained in this trial can best be attributed to the severity of the illness affecting these patients gained some support from another study reported by Gelder *et al.* (1967). They reported that a less satisfactory response to treatment was found in severe agoraphobics than among moderately disturbed (out-patient) phobics.

Although Gelder and Marks did not provide the mean number of sessions of treatment given to the severe agoraphobics, it is apparent from the duration of the treatment (given approximately 3 times a week) that these patients required considerably more treatment than those described either by Lazarus (1963) or by Meyer and Crisp (1966) or by Hain *et al.* (1966). The suggestion made by Gelder and Marks that the slightly better outcome for patients who received behaviour therapy can be accounted for by the longer duration of treatment is not entirely consistent with the observations reported by Hain *et al.*, who found that there was no correlation in their group of patients between duration of treatment and therapeutic outcome. Wolpe (1964) himself, however, reported that 65 patients with complex neuroses needed an average of 54.8 treatment sessions, whereas 21 patients with simple neuroses only required an average of 14.9 sessions.

As in every study on the subject, both clinical and experimental, Gelder and Marks could find no evidence that symptom substitution constitutes a problem. They also emphasize, however, the difficulty encountered in selecting patients for behaviour therapy.

These psychiatrists recently added another field trial to their valuable investigations. Gelder *et al.* (1967) carried out a controlled inquiry into the comparative effectiveness of desensitization, individual psychotherapy, or group psychotherapy in the treatment of phobic states. Forty-two moderately disturbed phobic patients were treated on an out-patient basis by 1 of these 3 methods. The patient groups were carefully matched and consisted of the following cases: desensitization group—8 agoraphobics, 4 social phobics, 4 with specific phobias; group therapy—7 agoraphobics, 3 social phobias, 6 specific phobias; individual psychotherapy—7 agoraphobics, 3 social phobias. They summed up their major findings in this way:

All raters agreed that, of the 3 treatments, desensitization produced more patients whose symptoms improved at the end of treatment and follow-up.

Symptoms, especially the presenting phobias, improved faster with desensitization than with psychotherapy. After 6 months, desensitization patients had changed more significantly than others, but this difference diminished later as the patients in psychotherapy went on improving slowly. Only 2 patients lost their symptoms completely, both with desensitization. At follow-up the degree of improvement still tended to be greater in those who had been treated with desensitization, but the difference was no longer statistically significant.

Ratings of social adjustment were less sensitive and reliable than symptom ratings; however, greater and more rapid improvement occurred in work and leisure adjustment with desensitization . . . (pp. 71–72). The number of patients whose phobias "were rated much improved by 2 of 3 raters at the final rating were: desensitization 9/16; group therapy 2/16; individual therapy 3/10" (p. 60).

In assessing these results, it is important to note that the desensitization group was treated weekly for about 9 months and then reassessed 9 months later. The patients in group therapy received 18 months of treatment, and their results do not include a follow-up. The patients who received individual therapy were treated for a year and reassessed 6 months later. Gelder *et al.* (1967), commenting on their results, occasionally fail to take these differences fully into account.

Although the groups were well matched in particulars, it is a pity that only 10 patients were included in the individual therapy group. Perhaps the main weakness in this study is the crudity of the assessment measures (mostly 5-point rating scales), but this is a difficulty with which all research workers can sympathize.

In examining the outcome of this trial, it is worth remembering that many of the subsidiary measures (e.g. of obsessions, of the therapist's rating of depression) deal with minor problems (for these patients). It is no surprise, therefore, that the 3 treatment groups rarely differ in these respects. Neither desensitization nor psychotherapy can produce superior results with subsidiary problems which are slight to begin with—simply, there is little room, or need, for change. Finally, some of the authors' concluding comments are arguable. Nevertheless, Marks's and Gelder's investigations are the best field trials available and need to be studied.

Gillan (1971) recently completed an investigation into the comparative effectiveness of desensitization, psychotherapy, and relaxation therapy in the management of phobic patients. There were 8 patients in each group, and the effects of treatment were assessed by clinical ratings (independent, self, and therapists), psychometrics, and physiological indices. On all of the main clinical measures the desensitized patients were found to be significantly better; the patients treated by psychotherapy or relaxation showed little change. These results persisted at the 3-month follow-up.

Obler and Terwilliger (1970) were successful in obtaining discernible clinical improvements in all 15 monophobic (and neurologically impaired) children treated by *in vivo* desensitization. Only 3 of 15 untreated controls showed the same degree of improvement.

The report made by Meyer and Crisp (1966) is particularly interesting as it describes their experiences with the use of behaviour therapy in a general psychiatric department which offers a wide range of diagnostic and treatment services and which caters for a heterogeneous group of patients. They quote the results obtained with 54 cases of mixed neurotic and behaviour disorders ranging from agoraphobia to encopresis. A variety of behavioural methods was used, and desensitization was the most common. The overall improvement rate was 70 per cent in a mean of 25 sessions. Only 2 relapses were noted and both of these were successfully re-treated.

Hain *et al.* (1966) presented a similar report of their clinical experiences except that they used only desensitization therapy. The work was carried out in a general psychiatric department which resembles that in which the Meyer and Crisp treatment was conducted. All of the 27 patients treated by Hain *et al.* were diagnosed as suffering from psychoneuroses and the duration of their symptoms ranged from 4 months to 50 years, with a mean of 8.6 years. The major symptoms encountered in these patients were anxiety and phobias. Seventy-eight per cent of the patients showed symptomatic improvement. These figures are similar to those reported by Meyer and Crisp.

The mean number of sessions required to treat patients was 19; this figure is similar to Meyer's and Crisp's experience. Hain *et al.* found there was no correlation between the degree of improvement obtained and the duration of treatment. The greatest improvement (in addition to the removal of the presenting symptom) was found in occupational functioning. Once again, although it was sought, no evidence of symptom substitution was elicited. Like Meyer and Crisp, these authors make some interesting comments about the practical difficulties encountered in the routine use of behaviour therapy (e.g. the selection of patients, the assessment of improvement, and so on).

Naturally, it is not sufficient merely to state that behaviour therapy can successfully induce improvement in neurotic conditions, particularly anxiety states. Ideally one would like to know what the effective act in these types of treatment is. It has already been argued that a number of the variables involved in desensitization therapy are not capable of inducing these improvements in isolation. For example, there is evidence that sheer muscle relaxation cannot by itself produce therapeutic improvements. Similarly, the improvements cannot be attributed to suggestibility, nor to hypnosis.

A more serious possibility is the one raised in various forms by Cooper (1963), Meyer and Gelder (1963), and Murray (1962) among others. Pointing to the measure of success which can be obtained by other forms of treatment, it has been argued that the primary cause of the therapeutic improvements must be attributed to the patient–therapist relationship which develops during the course of treatment. However, if this were the main vehicle of change, then it would be difficult to account for the fact that in most studies behaviour therapy appears to be more effective than other types of treatment—or, indeed, for the success of automated desensitization. Fortunately, we have some direct and indirect evidence which puts us in a position to estimate the contribution made to the progress of the therapy by the relationship between the patient and the therapist.

It should be pointed out initially that the contribution made by the relationship almost certainly varies with the type of disorder under consideration. In some types of disorder, particularly those which are complex and long-lasting, the relationship seems to be of some significance. Examples of this type are provided by Meyer and Gelder (1963). In other disorders, however, such as enuresis, the relationship is of virtually no significance in determining the outcome of behavioural treatment.

Costello (1963) has drawn attention to an important difference between conventional types of psychotherapy and behaviour therapy. He points out that many psychotherapists actively encourage the patient to form a close and even dependent emotional relationship with the therapist. In behaviour therapy, this type of emotional bond is discouraged as it is considered to be a possible source of interference with the re-learning process.

Obviously the behaviour therapist requires the co-operation of his patients and avoids giving them cause for distrust or distress. It must also be recognized that the therapist is a potential and powerful source of social reinforcement (see Ferster, 1958). The therapist can facilitate the reduction of anxiety in a formal manner (by relaxation, etc.) or in an informal manner by verbal conditioning and reassurance. In the treatment of children he can reduce anxiety by directly comforting the patient (Bentler, 1962).

Commenting on this problem, Eysenck and Rachman (1965) say that "it is preferable, and indeed necessary, to analyse the effect of the relationship in learning-theory terms rather than in psychoanalytic or psychodynamic manner. Explanations which rely on the concepts of psychosexuality and/or unconscious motives and ideas cannot accommodate some of the available evidence. In particular, the results obtained in the treatment of enuresis defy explanation in dynamic terms. Similarly, it is impossible to speak of a transference or counter-transference effect in attempting to account for the successful reduction of neurotic disturbances in animals by means of direct comforting and soothing (see the work of Anderson and Parmenter, 1941; Masserman, 1943; Haslerud et al., 1954 for examples)."

One might also add the evidence on the experimental use of de-sensitization treatment for excessive fears in normal subjects. In many of these studies the extent and degree of the interaction between the therapist and the subject was minimal. Nevertheless, significant reductions in fear were regularly obtained. Moreover, in some studies, such as that reported by Lang et al. (1966), even though a positive relationship was formed between the therapist and the subject, little therapeutic change was produced except when systematic desensitization was conducted. In the pseudo-therapy group used by these workers, their subjects reported that they had in fact developed a positive relationship to their therapist. However, their fear of snakes was not significantly reduced despite the growth of this relationship. It should be mentioned, however, that Paul (1966) obtained some evidence of beneficial effects apparently emerging from the putative development of a relationship between the therapist and the subject. He noted that some subjects showed a measure of improvement which may have been attributable to their positive feelings for the pseudo-therapists.

It seems reasonable to conclude that "the chief therapeutic contribution is made by the deliberate and systematic inhibition or extinction of the neurotic habit patterns—by deliberately facilitating the learning process" (Eysenck and Rachman, 1965). Direct evidence in support of this conclusion can be found in the number of case reports. Wolpe (1963) described in detail the treatment of a patient suffering from travel phobias and demonstrated the close correspondence between the stages completed in the desensitization of the travel hierarchy and the actual changes in the behaviour of the patient outside the consulting room (see also Clark, 1963).

In 1963 Wolpe attempted to quantify the relationships between the amount of training (learning trials) and the development of the learned reaction; he was able to demonstrate some interesting differences between what he called proximation phobias and other phobias. He found, for example, that "in claustrophobias and phobias in which anxiety arises with increasing proximity to a feared object" only a small number of practice trials (i.e. desensitization presentations of the scene) were required to reduce the anxiety experienced at a far distance from the feared object. As the feared object is approached, however, an increasing number of practice trials is required. This positively accelerating curve is a familiar feature of many learning processes. In the case of agoraphobias and other phobias which increase in intensity with the number of objects involved, the initial items on the hierarchy may be difficult to overcome (i.e. may require many practice trials). In this case the learning curve corresponds to a negatively accelerating function and the three cases of this type required a large number of scene presentations in order to cope with the initial items in the hierarchical list.

Translated into clinical practice this means that agoraphobias, for example, require a great deal of desensitization treatment before they can be helped to make the initial break-out of their encapsulated circles.

Once they have succeeded in moving beyond the restriction imposed by their phobic reactions, their progress tends to be fairly rapid and can be achieved with considerably less effort than that which has gone into the initial attempts to get the person moving again.

Apart from their contribution to determining the effective mechanisms in desensitization, these quantitative findings of Wolpe's show how therapeutic actions and reactions can be measured. Furthermore, they indicate how the lawful progression of the therapeutic learning process can be brought under close examination. The accumulation of further quantified observations of this type is desirable, and it is to be hoped that eventually we may be in the position to make reasonably accurate prognoses for the various types of phobia. It should also be possible to make predictions about the expected speed of progression from session to session with different types of disorder and different types of patient.

An accurate estimation of the clinical effects of the two newest techniques for reducing anxiety, flooding ("implosion") and modelling, must await the accumulation of more evidence. Theoretical expectations and experimental findings both give grounds for the highest degree of optimism. There is, moreover, a reasonable hope that these methods may reduce treatment time and effort by a considerable margin.

CHAPTER 11

BEHAVIOURAL TREATMENTS

ALTHOUGH desensitization is the most extensively used behavioural technique, considerable numbers of patients have been treated with aversion therapy or reinforcement therapy (operant conditioning techniques). Aversion therapy (Rachman and Teasdale, 1969) is used predominantly for the treatment of behaviour disorders in which the patient's conduct is undesirable but self-reinforcing (e.g. alcoholism and sexual disorders). The treatment is designed to bring about a necessary connection between the undesirable behaviour and some form of unpleasant stimulation, or to make the unpleasant stimulation a consequence of the undesirable behaviour. It is intended that the connection between the undesirable behaviour and the unpleasantness will develop to the point where it brings about a cessation of the target behaviour. Because of the appetitive characteristics of the disorders usually treated with this method, it is often desirable to introduce other suitable forms of satisfying behaviour—preferably those which are incompatible with the target behaviour. There is a growing recognition of the importance of generating alternate, satisfying forms of behaviour. Indeed, some authorities are now of the opinion that the aversion treatment is merely the first stage in the therapeutic programme; it is felt that the suppression of behaviour achieved by aversive stimulation should be regarded as temporary and that the therapist should use this period of non-responsiveness to identify and generate incompatible forms of behaviour.

Alcoholism is frequently treated by chemical aversion therapy and, in the well-conducted studies, the abstinence rate at 1 year is in the region of 60%. The relapse rate continues to be a problem but may be cut back by the inclusion of booster treatments. The majority of relapses occur within a year of treatment termination. Patients with cohesive backgrounds and stable personalities probably respond better than other types of patient. In addition, the strength of the patient's desire for change is positively related to treatment outcome. Although there is evidence that this form of treatment is frequently effective in substantially reducing alcoholism, it is not definitive. There are numerous evaluative problems of a complex nature which remain to be resolved, and we still require conclusive evidence that aversion therapy contributes more to the treatment process than the non-specific factors involved in general treatment and rehabilitation. Chemical aversion therapy has also been used to a limited extent in the treatment of sexual disorders. Some successes have been recorded, but homosexual patients do not respond well.

Electrical aversion therapy has been employed with apparent success in the treatment of transvestites, fetishists, homosexuals, exhibitionists, and the like, but the total number of cases reported is not yet large. In their 1964 report, McGuire and Vallance found that of their 39 patients treated by electrical methods, the 14 men with sexual disorders showed the best outcome. No fewer than 10 responded well to the treatment. An important series of cases was described by Marks and Gelder (1967), Marks et al. (1970). Despite the absence of a conventional control group the work reported with these patients provides persuasive evidence of the effectiveness of electrical aversion therapy. The transvestite patients did remarkably well but the trans-sexualists did not show much progress. The clinical outcome with the transvestite patients was exceptionally good and was maintained for at least 2 years with little change (Marks et al., 1970). The clinical improvement observed in 9 out of 10 of the transvestite patients was usually associated with positive attitudinal changes, psychophysiological changes, and alterations in sexual fantasies.

In a small-scale study on homosexual patients, Bancroft (1966) obtained only moderate success with electrical aversion. In a later publication he reported the comparative effectiveness of this technique and of desensitization (Bancroft, 1971). Although there was not a great deal to choose between the 2 methods in terms of clinical outcome, Bancroft expressed an understandable preference for desensitization.

Feldman and MacCulloch (1965) obtained encouraging results with 19 homosexual patients using electrical stimulation in an avoidance-conditioning paradigm. In a later report, Feldman (1968) stated that their early successes were being maintained and without altering their bold selection procedure they had completed treatment on 43 patients. At the end of a 1-year follow-up period, 25 patients were improved, 11 were failures, and 7 had defected from treatment.

Ten exhibitionists were treated with electrical aversion by Evans in 1968. Six months after treatment all of his patients were improved but 2 still exhibit themselves occasionally. In all it can be said that electrical aversion therapy has achieved its most encouraging results in the treatment of sexual disorders. The effects of this treatment in the management of alcoholism are equivocal.

In small-scale exploratory studies, MacCulloch et al. (1966) and McGuire and Vallance (1964) had discouraging results in the electrical treatment of alcoholism. On the other hand, Blake (1965, 1967) had a relatively good outcome with 59 (class 1 and class 2 patients). Of the 37 patients who received aversion therapy combined with relaxation training, 59% were abstinent or improved at the 1-year follow-up period. Of the 22 patients who received electrical treatment without supplementary relaxation training, 50% were abstinent or improved at 1 year.

McCance and McCance (1969) gave an unduly pessimistic impression of the outcome of their research into the effects of electrical aversion treatment with 78 alcoholics. Forty-five patients received aversion therapy and 33 had group therapy. Despite the conclusions stated by the authors, their results do give some slight encouragement for the view that aversion therapy yielded slightly better long-term results than either group psychotherapy or the routine ward treatment. However, a firm conclusion is precluded because of some problems in the analysis of the data (e.g. odd combinations of categories so that the amount of change can be classified into 1 of 5 grades—of which only 2 are used in the data analysis, etc.). Another possible explanation for their relatively barren outcome is the small number of aversion sessions given to the patients. This drawback is unlikely to be taken too seriously as the sheer amount of treatment provided is comparable with that given by Blake, who, it will be remembered, obtained far more encouraging results.

Apart from possible differences in technique, the conflicting results obtained by McCance and by Blake may be attributable to differences in the composition of their patient populations. In the chemical aversion treatment of this condition, it is certainly the case that the patients' biographical, personal, and sociological backgrounds are important prognostic factors.

The undue pessimism of McCance is matched by the excessive optimism of Vogler *et al.* (1970), who treated 73 male, voluntary, alcoholic patients who had been persistently overdrinking for at least 3 years. Their patients were given intensive treatment (20 sessions) over a 10-day period involving approximately 400 administrations of shock. Their results appear to show that the electrical aversion treatment produces slightly longer periods of abstinence than control treatments. The authors also emphasize the apparent effectiveness of booster treatments which, they claim, reduce the relapse rate and increase the duration of abstinence. Unfortunately, their affirmative conclusions appear to give insufficient weight to the fact that the patients who received the booster treatments were "self-selected" and might have been those most likely to improve under any circumstances. For example, it could be argued that they were more highly motivated to improve than were those patients who did not return for further treatment. A second cause for caution in the interpretation of the results is the apparent absence of a significant difference between the patients who received orthodox treatment and those who received a control procedure involving the random administration of shock ("sham" treatment). The absence of differences between these groups suggests that the treatment effect must be attributable in large measure to non-specific therapeutic factors of the type discussed by Rachman and Teasdale (1969). In a discursive consideration of aversion therapy these writers drew attention to the puzzling theoretical problems which are unresolved, and their review of the evidence on the clinical effectiveness of the treatment was encouraging but cautious. They stated that their "evaluation of the available evidence is that aversion therapy is probably effective but we have been unable to satisfy ourselves beyond all doubt. Nevertheless, at present, there is sufficient evidence to justify the judicious and enquiring use of aversion therapy."

Reinforcement Therapy

The particular strength of Skinner's work (1957, 1959) is that it provides a method which enables one to generate and shape new responses. Crudely speaking, this is achieved by rewarding appropriate and desirable responses and by withholding rewards when inappropriate or undesirable responses occur. "Operant behaviour usually affects the environment and generates stimuli which feed back to the organism. Some feedback may have the effects identified by the layman as reward and punishment. Any consequence of behaviour which is rewarding or, more technically, *reinforcing*, increases the probability of further responding" (Skinner, 1959).

The constructive power of operant procedures has been of special value in the management of behaviour problems which fall into the category known as "deficit disorders" (Eysenck and Rachman, 1965). Since Skinnerian-minded psychologists first turned their attention to human behaviour disorders some 17 years ago, they have carried out a startling amount of clinical work and research. With varying degrees of success, they have applied themselves to the problems of handicapped children (e.g. Bucher and Lovaas, 1970; Birnbrauer and Wolf 1965), echolalic speech (Risley and Wolf, 1967), chronic psychotic patients (e.g. Ayllon and Azrin, 1968; Atthowe and Krasner, 1968), delinquent behaviour (Cohen, 1969), and numerous other matters.

It is regrettably true that relatively few of the extensive therapeutic claims made on behalf of operant procedures have yet been subjected to the rigours of a formal clinical trial in the manner widely accepted to be desirable (e.g. see the discussions provided by Bandura, 1969; Krasner, 1970; Davison, 1969), Many Skinnerian workers explicitly reject the desirability or value of standard clinical trials and prefer to demonstrate the functional effectiveness of particular interventions or procedures. Some of the methods employed to demonstrate the functional relationships between behaviour and the conditions controlling such behaviour are discussed by Sidman (1960). Although these "scientific tactics" are of undoubted value, it is far from certain that they provide a suitable substitute for more conventional experimental investigations of therapeutic procedures. Some of the drawbacks to the

Skinnerian methods of experimentation and demonstration are mentioned by Bandura (1969). They include the difficulties involved in studying behaviour which is to some extent irreversible, the statistical problems inherent in some of the Skinnerian techniques (including the partial or outright rejection of statistical techniques by some Skinnerian workers), and the difficulties involved in determining the relative contributions of different treatment variables. Other potential difficulties include the effect of changes in manipulative conditions on the behaviour itself, and, lastly, the problems which arise in attempting to recover an original baseline of the morbid behaviour under consideration. Despite this seemingly formidable list of difficulties, the Skinnerian approach to the rules of evidence concerning behaviour change can be sufficiently persuasive to merit the introduction of new techniques. On the other hand, attempts entirely to replace the accepted procedures of therapeutic assessment by exclusively Skinnerian methods would be unwelcome and unlikely to succeed.

This is not the place for a detailed review of the large number of experiments on operant methods pertinent to abnormal psychology. Nor do I intend to deal with those applications of the operant procedures which would not ordinarily be thought of as psychological treatment, i.e. modification of behaviour in a classroom, conditioning of normal verbal responses in student subjects the education of retarded children, and the like. Although all of these psychological applications are relevant to the extent that they describe intended and deliberate modifications of behaviour, they are better regarded as techniques of management rather than of treatment. In passing, it is worth noting that the remarkable advances achieved with operant procedures in the training and education of handicapped and retarded children is one of the most impressive contributions of applied psychology in recent times. Incidentally, the effectiveness of the training procedures can be "functionally" demonstrated readily and speedily; for example, the ease with which handicapped children can be taught self-help behaviour within a matter of days is unchallenged and easily repeatable evidence of the functional relationship between the training conditions and the consequent behaviour. Certainly, the power of the arguments advocating these training procedures would be strengthened by the execution of field trials which include "non-treated" control groups, but in the present example insistence on conventional control procedures may be an indication of sheer obstinacy.

For present purposes, the trend of the evidence can be illustrated by reference to research on the conditioning of speech and on the rehabilitation of chronic psychotic patients. An early report of an attempt to restore speech in chronic schizophrenic patients was described by Isaacs *et al.* (1960). The first of the 2 patients whom they retrained had been mute for 14 years at the time the experiment took place. He had been attending group therapy sessions with other chronic patients who were, however, able to speak. The patient had made no progress and appeared to be indifferent to the various rewards which had been offered to him, but at one session the experimenter accidentally dropped a packet of chewing gum. Observing the patient's reaction to the gum, the experimenter decided to use it as the main source of reinforcement. By a process of patient successive approximations he was able to get the patient to use first one word, then groups of words, and, finally, sentences. Their second patient, who had also been mute for 14 years, received similar treatment. He also made some progress but unfortunately his newly restored verbal behaviour did not generalize to a sufficiently wide range of situations and people. This failure to generalize the re-acquired speech was also noted in an experiment by Wilson and Walters (1966). Three groups of 4 regressed mute-like schizophrenic patients took part in this experiment. One group acted as controls while the patients in the second group were conditioned to model an increase in word output to the presentation of slides. A third group of patients was given modelling plus the addition of monetary rewards for correct responses. While the verbal output of the 2 groups of patients who were rewarded showed an increase in the experimental situation, this failed to generalize in the form of increased responsiveness in other situations. A disappointing result was also reported by Robertson in 1958 when he unsuccessfully attempted to shape the behaviour of 3 mute catatonic patients. He ascribed the failure of this attempt to the fact that it was difficult to find a suitable reward for which these patients would work. Consequently his attention was directed towards the effects of different kinds of reward in modifying the verbal behaviour of schizophrenic patients (Robertson, 1961). After studying 24 patients he showed that they responded differently to various types of reward—some responded favourably to praise while others responded to concrete rewards. Kennedy (1964) was more successful in her attempt to reinforce the speech content of 3 paranoid patients. When the patients emitted delusional material they were ignored and when they spoke normally they received prompt attention and other social reinforcement. Marked improvements were noted, but it is not possible to ascribe these changes solely to the conditioning procedures as the patients were at the same time receiving drug treatments. These early findings have now been extended, and recent accounts vary between those which report only slightly successful results and those which are extremely productive. Not surprisingly, some patients failed to respond at all. On the other hand, some patients show a gratifying and substantial response with relatively little therapeutic effort. These improvements have sometimes been observed to exceed the type and amount of training which has been given, and therefore provide evidence of non-specific and sometimes wide-ranging improvements not solely attributable to the operant conditioning procedures *per se*. As might have been predicted from the early work and on general principles, the successful restoration of speech within the training situation is not always followed by a reappearance of natural speech in other situations, but, it should be said, specific steps can be taken to increase the likelihood of transfer taking place.

Working with children, Ferster and de Meyer (1961) made a prolonged study of the behaviour of 2 autistic patients in an operant conditioning environment (specially constructed). They demonstrated, as Lindsley (1956, 1960) had done with adult patients, that it is possible to shape the behaviour of these extremely disturbed children in a range of stimulating conditions, and they also obtained information about the effects of different reinforcement schedules and types of reinforcer. Having shown that the behaviour of autistic children could be brought under some measure of experimental control, the thread was then taken up by a number of clinicians. In 1962 Salzinger attempted to condition speech in a 4-year-old autistic boy. The child was seen daily for 6 months, and having started with the ability to produce only grunts, eventually acquired the ability to pronounce 12 words appropriately. In 1965, Salzinger added a report of another 4-year-old child with whom he had more success. Unlike the first child, the second patient generalized his newly shaped speech to novel situations and also began using sentences. It should be noted, however, that, prior to treatment, this child had the remnants of some speech and was able to pronounce a few words. Among his other comments on these 2 formidable undertakings, Salzinger mentions the problems which arose when attempting to use reward training over a period of more than a year with very young children. Similar problems were encountered by Kerr *et al.* (1965) in attempting to train vocalizations in a severely disturbed 3-year-old mute child.

Some of the most encouraging results have been reported by Lovaas (1966) and his colleagues (e.g. Bucher and Lovaas, 1970), who have attempted to provide a total rehabilitation procedure for autistic and other severely disturbed children. They have obtained some striking successes and report that it has also been possible to generate and shape speech even in a small number of children who had been formerly mute. Risley and Wolf (1967) have reported particular success in the treatment of echolalic children, and their concise account of the technique employed is especially valuable.

Much of the published work on the subject is summarized in Table 5. One of the interesting trends to emerge is that echolalic children respond better than mutes (a finding consistent with our own experience at the Maudsley Hospital and the Institute of Psychiatry over a period of 4 or 5 years). In Table 5 it will be seen that of the 30 children described, 14 had no useful speech before treatment. After treatment 6 were still without speech, 6 had less than 25 words, and 3 had 25 plus labels. On the other hand, echolalic children do well and respond quickly. The remaining children require a great deal of time and training effort. An unfortunate omission in many of the published reports is the absence of satisfactory data on the diagnosis, intelligence, and baseline speech of the children being described. Inadequacies of this and other types of information make it difficult to assess the clinical value of operant speech training in these types of children—particularly as approximately one-quarter might have been expected to acquire speech without specific training (Rutter, 1965). It would also be extremely useful to know what the long-term state of these children was—in other words, does it make any substantial difference to the course of their lives even if the treatment is to some extent successful at the time when it is provided?

TABLE 5

THE EFFECTS OF OPERANT SPEECH TRAINING (COMPILED WITH P. TILBY)

Author	Date	Sex	Age	Diagnosis	Initial level	Outcome	Time
1. Lovaas	1966	M	6	Childhood schizophrenia	No speech	Regular imitation	6 days per week, 7 hr per day for 26 days
		M	6	Childhood schizophrenia	Infrequent vowels	No details of further work given	
2. Wolf et al.	1964	M	3½	Childhood schizophrenia	Echolalia	Like normal 5-year-old	2–3 years
3. Risley and Wolf (Johnston later)	1967	M	7	Autistic? Retarded?	Echolalia	Appropriate use of phrases. Some spontaneous conversation	No information
4. Sloane et al.	1968	M	8	Severely retarded	Echolalia	No information	
		M	10	Childhood autism	Echolalia	Labelling stage assumed	
		F	12	Childhood autism	Echolalia	40 words	
		M	3 yr 7 m	Retarded	No speech	60 single words, 35 2-word phrases, 25 3-word phrases	About 8 months
		M	4 yr 7 m	Very retarded	10–15 single words	Increase from 100 to 600 responses per 90-min session	7 months
		M	7 yr 5 m	Retarded and autistic	24 tacts, 12 mands, 6 social responses	Regular naming. Language no longer a problem	
		F	3 yr 3 m	?	0–4 words. Sounds		
		F	4 yr 8 m	Retarded	High verbal rate, poor articulation	Little change	
		F	4	Brain damage	No words	Most speech sounds. 10 words	1 month
5. Salzinger et al.	1965	M	3½	Organic. IQ 32	No words, no imitation	Increase in vocalization. 4–5 clear words	150 hr
		M	3 yr 10 m	Behaviour disturbance. I.Q. normal	Some words. Response to commands	Sentences with variety of grammatical constructions	
6. Hewett	1965	M	4½	Autistic	2 words ever; no speech	150 words, used meaningfully	14 months
7. Weiss and Born	1967	M	7½	?	Echolalia	Sentences, but no generalization outside	9 months approx.
8. Schell et al.	1967	M	4½	Autistic	No speech	Few words, response to commands	45 sessions

TABLE 5 (cont.)

Author	Date	Sex	Age	Diagnosis	Initial level	Outcome	Time
9. Cook and Adams	1966	M	13	Retarded	2 words ever, no speech	Increase in sounds	12 hr
10. Jensen and Womack	1967	M	6	Retarded	No speech	Increase in syllables	20 sessions
		M	13	Retarded	3 words per day	76 words per session	
		M	7	Autistic	Single words	Words combined with generalization	
11. Wetzel et al.	1966	M	6	Retarded	Echolalia	100 names; 70–80 commands followed. Initiates simple requests	20 sessions
12. Blake and Moss	1967	F	4	? (Mute)	No speech	2 words	
13. Kerr et al.	1965	F	3	Retarded (mute)	Grunts	Increased vocalization	
14. Hingten et al.	1967	M	6	Autistic	Mute	18 words	46 sessions
		F	5	Autistic	Mute	11 words	46 sessions
15. Evans	1969	M	6	Autistic	Random noise	200 words; spontaneous speech	45 sessions
16. Brawley et al.	1969	M	5	Autistic	Random noise	Imitation of sounds	26 sessions
		M	7	Brain damage?	Echolalic	Spontaneous speech	21 sessions
		M	7	Autistic	Virtually mute	Descriptive speech	20 sessions

An observation made at the Maudsley Hospital but seldom mentioned elsewhere is what we have come to call reactivation. By this is meant the "spontaneous" reappearance of speech known to have been previously present in the child's repertoire (i.e. prior to the onset of the illness) but which has not featured in the training programme or on the ward. It seems that in some way the experience of the speech-training conditioning exercises may produce success not only in the particular words which feature in the training sessions but may also serve to reactivate speech which was previously present but has become dormant. Improvements in general behaviour are also noted to occur as a "side-effect" of speech training.

At the risk of over-simplifying, the present position can be summarized in this way. There seems to be sufficient evidence, both experimental and clinical, to enable us to say that it is possible to condition speech even in severely disturbed patients. Particularly good results can be obtained with echolalics, but failures have also been reported, particularly with mute patients. Even though the generation or regeneration of speech often can be accomplished with present operant conditioning techniques, it is sometimes extremely time-consuming. And it is not necessarily used by the patient outside the training situations—even where transfer experiences are arranged.

Token Economies

Following Lindsley's (1956, 1960) early attempts to apply the procedures and ideas of operant conditioning to clinical problems, Ayllon and his colleagues made the first attempts to apply Skinnerian ideas in psychiatric wards (e.g. Ayllon and Michael, 1959; Ayllon and Haughton, 1962; Ayllon, 1963; Ayllon and Azrin, 1968). Their pioneering work was an important development for a variety of reasons, including the fact that this was one of the earliest attempts to apply Skinnerian ideas directly to the behaviour of human beings. Ayllon and his colleagues made systematic attempts to use the procedures of positive reinforcement, extinction, satiation, and the like in modifying the behaviour of chronic schizophrenic patients; and by an imaginative use of these techniques they were able to obtain striking improvements in numbers of severely ill patients. Some of their earliest successes were obtained in overcoming feeding problems, hoarding, and tantrum behaviour. After a short period during which this work seemed to be making little impact, schemes using reinforcement therapy based on Ayllon's work mushroomed in the United States. In 1968 Krasner was able to list approximately 110 token economy programmes in operation in 2 continents. They included programmes designed to assist retarded subjects, delinquents, psychotics, and others. The aim of these operant programmes is always to develop adaptive behaviour in the subjects which will lead to social and other reinforcement from people in the "natural environment". More generally, the programmes attempt to increase the social and other skills of the subject. In operation, these token economies involve the selection of desirable behaviour patterns to be reinforced, the administration of tokens for successful performance of the behaviour, and an exchange system in which the tokens can be used to obtain material or other rewards. Unadaptive behaviour is weakened by ensuring that it is no longer reinforced.

Although some ingenious programmes have been devised and extensive results claimed, there is an absence of conventional evidence demonstrating the clinical effectiveness of these programmes. For example, Marks et al. (1967), while demonstrating that reinforcement (token) therapy improved the behaviour of chronic hospitalized patients, found that more orthodox "relationship therapy" produced comparable changes. In his recent review of the subject, Davison (1969) expressed less than the customary enthusiasm for these procedures but nevertheless concluded that they have been shown, beyond doubt, to be capable of markedly influencing abnormal behaviour. Bandura's (1969) thoughtful review concludes that "contingent reinforcement" has been demonstrated to be a highly effective means of modifying abnormal behaviour and that this is "most impressively revealed by studies in which tenacious deviant behaviour is successively eliminated and re-instated by varying its social consequences . . ." (p. 283). Bandura goes on to point out that these findings emphasize "the influential role played by environmental contingencies in the regulation of behaviour". If anything, the danger of these studies is that they over-emphasize the depth and extent of environmental control of abnormal behaviour. There is a further implication, erroneous of course, that if one is successful in modifying abnormal behaviour by a conditioning procedure (for example) this demonstrates that the abnormal behaviour was originally produced by a similar conditioning procedure. The specific contribution made by the explicit reinforcers is too often assumed rather than demonstrated. For example, token programmes rarely allow for the general improvements observed when new schemes of any type are introduced, nor do they allow for the therapeutic effects of increased social and other stimulation on a population of chronic or backward patients (see Chapter 9). The relative insensitivity of some patients is not well understood—some of them show little change despite tokens and other reinforcers while others show marked changes even in the absence of denoted reinforcers. The problem of transfer of skills or behaviour changes from the "economy" to other settings requires elucidation. One last limitation should be mentioned. The tendency to over-emphasize the importance of environmental contingencies in the regulation and maintenance of abnormal behaviour often has the unfortunate result of making the various types of disorder virtually indistinguishable. Carried to extremes, the operant view of abnormal behaviour would reduce one to expecting and, indeed, predicting that all abnormal behaviour, produced and maintained as it is largely by "social reinforcement", should be similar if not identical.

The introduction of operant conditioning into the clinical field has entended and enlightened our view of abnormal behaviour and also provided us with a powerful technology for modifying such behaviour. It is particularly valuable in the management of deficit disorders because it enables one to generate and maintain new behaviour. For this reason it has achieved its most impressive successes so far in the training of retarded and handicapped people. Thus far it has had less success with the surplus reactions which are mainly of the neurotic variety (Eysenck and Rachman, 1965). In the management of chronic psychotic patients, substantial and important improvements in behaviour can be obtained, but there is still considerable resistance to accepting the view that these procedures are essentially rehabilitative in nature. The introduction of these methods into clinical psychology has already made an impact on institutional care and this influence can be expected to deepen and spread in the coming years. Recently completed research (Krasner, 1970) also encourages the hope that operant conditioning procedures may prove to be of some value in the management and retraining of delinquents. One of the major, latent benefits of operant programmes may well be the new optimism and energetic interest which they engender in the custodially minded staff of the institutions concerned.

CHAPTER 12

SOME CONCLUDING REMARKS

THE subject of this book is psychological treatment but it must be remembered that many, perhaps most, psychiatric patients receive other forms of treatment—mainly supportive therapy and drugs, but also ECT and so on. In addition, patients receive informal non-professional psychological treatment from friends and relations. The value of this type of support, advice, and encouragement is acknowledged but dimly understood. Patients also benefit, as do we all, from fortunate "life events".

These potentially therapeutic factors probably play a part in the occurrence of the spontaneous remissions which are characteristic of psychiatric conditions, particularly those of the neurotic type. These natural improvements are not uncaused, and an increased appreciation of their action would be of great value. The fact of their occurrence, in addition to providing therapists with some basis for the optimism required in their daily efforts, also provides a perspective against which therapeutic research should be assessed. If the spontaneous remission index is to continue to provide a useful perspective it will need to be revised for improved accuracy as the crude rates will become misleading rather than enlightening.

Although it is not possible to demonstrate that psychotherapy is effective in the sense of that term as used in this book, it remains open for advocates of this type of treatment to show that it has other uses or values. For example, it could be argued that even if psychotherapy is not effective in dealing with the patient's disorder, it does provide him with a measure of comfort while the natural processes of remission take their course. The partly supported claim that numbers of patients (but by no means all of them) actually enjoy undergoing psychotherapy is consistent with this view. Another possibility is that psychotherapy, although unable to surpass the natural remission rate, may expedite it. This possibility cannot, of course, be considered for psychoanalytic therapy as it usually exceeds 2 years (during which period a majority of remissions occur). There is a further alternative and one which has numerous adherents. It is said that psychotherapy brings about constructive changes in personality, but until recently this seemingly extravagant claim had not been examined in a recognizably scientific manner. The work of the Rogerian group has already revealed some of the expected complexities of this research, and on current evidence all but the most limited and specific claims must be regarded as excessive. It may be that psychotherapeutic procedures, even of the analytic type, do produce personality changes. Once that first claim is established, one will need to know if such changes are therapeutic or not. Then, whether they are efficient, and so on. The advocacy and practice of psychotherapy, if based on the justification of personality changes, can only be thought of as a gamble. On present knowledge, it is not a well-chosen chance. Lastly, if the purpose of psychotherapy is to produce personality changes, then the patient needs to have this explained before agreeing to undertake the course. It might also be proper, if psychoanalysis is to be used, to point out to the prospective patient that on the basis of the results of the American analytic survey, his symptoms are unlikely to change.

In like manner, behaviour therapists should explain to their prospective patients that although their symptoms are likely to be reduced or (hopefully) eliminated, no changes in personality can be promised.

The desire to integrate behaviour therapy and psychodynamic forms of therapy appears to be fairly commonly held. It has, indeed, been the subject of a small, special conference (Porter, 1968). Although a majority of the invited participants appeared to share this desire, some of the proponents of behaviour therapy expressed less enthusiasm. Krasner, in particular, expressed his doubts about the desirability of what he called "bridge building", and argued that attempts of this type might tend to obscure the real and important differences between the 2 approaches (1968, p. 326). If anything, he appeared to lean more in the direction of "bridge bombing" than "bridge building".

It would appear that there are two primary questions which need to be answered. In the first place, is such an integration desirable? Secondly, even if desirable, is such an integration feasible?

Although there is a general and entirely understandable desire that scientific controversies be resolved promptly and satisfactorily, it need not follow that the resolution must involve an integration of opposing points of view. One would need to demonstrate that an integration between opposing views is of potential value—either on theoretical grounds or for practical reasons, or preferably due to both of these considerations. My own view is similar to Krasner's: such an integration is theoretically undesirable because it would obscure the fundamental and important differences between the 2 approaches. There are major differences on the origins and maintenance of abnormal behaviour. The explanations of therapeutic change are vastly different; for example, on the role of insight, the therapeutic relationship, selection for treatment, the conditions of learning. Even the purpose and evaluation of treatment are divergent. On a practical level, a combination of approaches would need to be demonstrably more effective than either form of treatment administered separately. There are, however, good grounds for believing that this is an improbable outcome.

We do not have satisfactory evidence to support the claim that psychotherapy is effective. It would seem, therefore, that those psychologists and psychiatrists who advocate and/or practise psychotherapy carry the burden of having to demonstrate the value of their views and practices. A combination of behavioural and psychodynamic methods would only be justifiable if it could be shown that psychotherapy is even partly effective. In the absence of proof of this type, no useful purpose would be achieved by watering down the behavioural techniques.

The burden of producing a satisfactory case for the continued use of psychotherapy rests with those who advocate it. A similar burden rests with those people who advocate a combination of psychotherapy and behaviour therapy.

BIBLIOGRAPHY

ANDERSON, O. and PARMENTER, R. (1941) *A Long-term Study of Experimental Neuroses in the Sheep and Dog*, Psychosom. Med. Monogr., Suppl.

ANKER, J. and WALSH, R. (1961) Group psychotherapy, activity program and group structure in the treatment of chronic schizophrenics, *J. Consult. Psychol.* **25**, 476–81.

ASHCRAFT, C. and FITTS, W. (1964) Self-concept change in psychotherapy, *Psychother. Theor. Res. Pract.* **1**, 115–18.

ATTHOWE, J. and KRASNER, L. (1968) A report on the application of contingent reinforcement procedures on a chronic ward, *J. Abnorm. Psychol.* **73**, 37–43.

AUERBACH, A. (1961) A survey of selected literature on psychotherapy of schizophrenia, in *Psychotherapy of Schizophrenia* (ed. A. Scheften), Thomas, Springfield.

AUSUBEL, D. (1958) *Drug Addiction*, Random House, New York.

AYLLON, T. (1963) Intensive treatment of psychotic behavior, *Behav. Res. Ther.* **1**, 53–61.

AYLLON, T. and AZRIN, N. (1968) *The Token Economy*, Wiley, New York.

AYLLON, T. and HAUGHTON, F. (1962) Control of the behavior of schizophrenic patients by food, *J. Exp. Anal. Behav.* **5**, 343–52.

AYLLON, T. and MICHAEL, J. (1959) The psychiatric nurse as a behavioral engineer, *J. Exp. Anal. Behav.* **2**, 323–34.

AZIMA, H. and WITTKOWER, E. (1956) Gratifications of basic needs in schizophrenia, *Psychiatry* **19**, 121–9.

BAEHR, G. (1954) The comparative effectiveness of individual psychotherapy and group psychotherapy, *J. Consult. Psychol.* **18**, 179–83.

BANCROFT, J. (1966) D.P.M. Dissert., Univ. of London.

BANCROFT, J. (1971) A comparative study of aversion and desensitization in the treatment of homosexuality, in *Behaviour Therapy in the 1970s* (eds. L. Burns and J. Worsley), Wright, Bristol.

BANDURA, A. (1969) *Principles of Behaviour Modification*, Holt, Reinhart & Winston, New York.

BANDURA, A. and MENLOVE, F. (1968) Factors determining vicarious extinction of avoidance behavior through symbolic modeling, *J. Pers. Soc. Psychol.* **8**, 99–108.

BARBOUR, R. F. and BEEDELL, C. J. (1955) The follow-up of a child guidance clinic population, *J. Ment. Sci.* **101**, 794–809.

BARENDREGT, J. T. (1961) *Research in Psychodiagnostics*, Mouton, Paris.

BARLOW, D., LEITENBERG, H., AGRAS, S. and WINCZE, J. (1969) The transfer gap in systematic desensitization, *Behav. Res. Ther.* **7**, 191–6.

BARRETT, C. (1969) Systematic desensitization versus implosive therapy, *J. Abnorm. Psychol.* **74**, 587–92.

163

BARRON, F. and LEARY, T. (1955) Changes in psychoneurotic patients with and without psychotherapy, *J. Consult. Psychol.* **19**, 239–45.

BELLAK, L. and LOEB, L. (1969) Psychoanalytic, psychotherapeutic, and generally psychodynamic studies, in *The Schizophrenic Syndrome* (eds. Bellak and Loeb), Grune & Stratton, New York.

BENDIG, A. (1962) Pitsburgh scale of social introversion–extraversion and emotionality, *J. Psychol.* **53**, 199–210.

BENNET, I. (1966) Changing concepts in insulin coma treatment, in *Biological Treatment of Mental Illness* (ed. M. Rinkel), Farrar, New York.

BENTLER, P. M. (1962) An infant's phobia treated with reciprocal inhibition therapy, *J. Child Psychol. Psychiat.* **3**, 185–9.

BERGIN, A. E. (1963) The effects of psychotherapy: negative results re-visited, *J. Counsel. Psychol.* **10**, 244–50.

BERGIN, A. E. (1966) Some implications of psychotherapy research for therapeutic practice, *J. Abnorm. Psychol.* **71**, 235–46.

BERGIN, A. E. (1967) Further comments on psychotherapy research, *Int. J. Psychiat.* **3**, 317–23.

BERGIN, A. E. (1970) The evaluation of therapeutic outcomes, in *Handbook of Psychotherapy and Behaviour Change* (eds. A. E. Bergin and S. Garfield), Wiley New York.

BIEBER, I. (ed.) (1962) *Homosexuality: A Psychoanalytic Study*, Basic Books, New York.

BIRNBRAUER, J. and WOLF, M. (1965) Controlling classroom behavior of retarded children with token reinforcement, *J. Exp. Child. Psychol.* **2**, 219–35.

BLAKE, B. G. (1965) The application of behaviour therapy to the treatment of alcoholism, *Behav. Res. Ther.* **3**, 75–85.

BLAKE, B. G. (1967) A follow-up of alcoholics treated by behaviour therapy, *Behav. Res. Ther.* **5**, 89–94.

BLAKE, P. and MOSS, L. (1967) The development of socialization skills in an electively mute child, *Behav. Res. Ther.* **5**, 349–56.

BOCKOVER, J. (1956) Moral treatment in American psychiatry, *J. Nerv. Ment. Dis.* **124**, 167–94.

BOULOUGOURIS, J., MARKS, I. M., and MARSET, P. (1971) Superiority of flooding (implosion) to desensitization for reducing pathological fear, *Behav. Res. Ther.* **9**, 7–16.

BOYER, L. and GIOVACCHINI, P. (1967) *Psychoanalytic Treatment of Schizophrenic and Characterological Disorders*, Science House Inc., New York.

BRAWLEY, E., HARRIS, F., ALLEN, K., FLEMING, R., and PETERSON, R. (1969) Behaviour modification of an autistic child, *Behav. Sci.* **14**, 87.

BRILL, A. A. (1944) *Freud's Contribution to Psychiatry*, Norton, New York.

BRILL, N. and BEEBE, G. (1955) *A Follow-up Study of War Neuroses*, Washington VA, Medical Monogr.

BRILL, N., KOEGLER, R., EPSTEIN, L., and FORGY, E. (1964) Controlled study of psychiatric outpatient treatment, *Arch. Gen. Psychiat.* **10**, 581–95.

BRODY, M. (1962) Prognosis and results of psychotherapy, in *Psychosomatic Medicine* (eds. J. Nodine and J. Moyer), Lea & Febiger, Philadelphia.

BUCHER, B. and LOVAAS, I. (1970) Operant procedures in behavior modification with children, in *Learning Approaches to Therapeutic Behavior Change* (ed. D. J. Levis), Aldine Press, Chicago.

BURNETT, A. and RYAN, E. (1963) The application of conditioning techniques in psychotherapy in a day-care treatment hospital (unpublished report).

CANTER, F. (1969) The future of psychotherapy with alcoholics, in *The Future of Psychotherapy* (ed. C. Frederick), Little, Brown & Co., Boston.

CAPPON, D. (1964) Results of psychotherapy, *Br. J. Psychiat.* 110, 34–45.

CARKHUFF, R. and TRUAX, C. (1965) Lay mental health counselling, *J. Consult. Psychol.* 29, 426–31.

CARTWRIGHT, D. S. (1956) Note on "changes in psychoneurotic patients with and without psychotherapy", *J. Consult. Psychol.* 20, 403–4.

CARTWRIGHT, D. S. and VOGEL, J. (1960) A comparison of changes in psychoneurotic patients during matched periods of therapy and no-therapy, *J. Consult. Psychol.* 24, 121–7.

CARTWRIGHT, R. D. (1968) Psychotherapeutic processes, in *Annual Review of Psychology* (ed. P. Farnsworth), Ann. Rev. Inc., Palo Alto.

CLARK, D. F. (1963) Treatment of a monosymptomatic phobia by systematic desensitization, *Behav. Res. Ther.* 1, 89–104.

CLEIN, E. (1959) A follow-up of non-attenders at the Maudsley Hospital. Dissert., London University.

COHEN, R. (1969) The effects of group interaction and progressive hierarchies on test anxiety, *Behav. Res. Ther.* 7, 15–26.

COLLINGWOOD, T., HEFELE, T., MUEHLBERG, N. and DRASGOW, J. L. (1970) Toward identification of the therapeutically facilitative factor, *J. Clin. Psychol.* 26, 119–20,

COOK, C. and ADAMS, H. (1966) Modification of verbal vehaviour in speech deficient children, *Behav. Res. Ther.* 4, 265–71.

COOKE, G. (1966) The efficacy of two desensitization procedures: an analogue study, *Behav. Res. Ther.* 4, 17–24.

COOPER, J. E. (1963) A study of behaviour therapy in 30 psychiatric patients, *Lancet* 1, 411–15.

COOPER, J. E. (1969) Lecture, Institute of Psychiatry.

COOPER, J. E., GELDER, M. G. and MARKS, I. M. (1965) Results of behaviour therapy in 77 psychiatric patients. *Br. Med. J.* 1, 1222–5.

COSTELLO, C. G. (1963) Behaviour therapy: criticisms and confusions, *Behav. Res. Ther.* 1, 159–62.

COSTELLO, C. G., and BELTON, G. P. (1970) Depression: treatment, in *Symptoms of Psychopathology* (ed. C. G. Costello), Wiley, New York.

COTLER, S. (1970) Sex differences and generalization of anxiety reduction with automated desensitization, *Behav. Res. Ther.* 8, 273–86.

COTLER, S. and GARLINGTON, W. (1969) The generalization of anxiety reduction following desensitization, *Behav. Res. Ther.* 7, 35–40.

COWDEN, R., ZAX, M. and SPROLES, J. (1956) Group psychotherapy in conjunction with a physical treatment, *J. Clin. Psychol.* 12, 53–56.

COWEN, E. and COOMBS, A. (1950) Follow-up of 32 cases treated by non-directive psychotherapy, *J. Abnorm. Psychol.* 45, 232–58.

CREAK, E. (1963) Childhood psychosis, *Br. J. Psychiat.* 109, 84–89.

CREMERIUS, J. (1962) *Die Beurteilung des Behandlungserfolges in der Psychotherapie*, Springer Verlag, Berlin.

CREMERIUS, J. (1969) Spatschicksale unbehandelter Neurosen, *Berliner Ärztekammer* 12, 389–92.

CRIGHTON, J. and JEHU, D. (1969) Treatment of exam anxiety, *Behav. Res. Ther.* 7, 245–8.

CROSS, H. J. (1964) The outcome of psychotherapy, *J. Consult. Psychol.* **28**, 413–17.

CROSSMAN, R. (1969) Speech of welcome to members of 19th International Congress of Psychology, *Bull. Br. Psychol. Soc.* **22**, 261–5.

CROWDER, D. and THORNTON, D. (1970) Effects of systematic desensitization programmed fantasy and bibliotherapy on a specific fear, *Behav. Res. Ther.* **8**, 35–42.

CROWNE, D. and STEPHENS, M. (1961) Self-acceptance and self-evaluative behaviour: a critique of methodology, *Psychol. Bull.* **58**, 104–21.

CURRAN, D. and GUTTMANN, E. (1949) *Psychological Medicine* (3rd edn.), Livingstone, Edinburgh.

CURRAN, D. and PARTRIDGE, M. (1955) *Psychological Medicine* (4th edn.), Livingstone, London.

CURRAN, D. and PARTRIDGE, M. (1963) *Psychological Medicine* (5th edn.), Livingstone, London.

CYTRYN, L., GILBERT, A. and EISENBERG, L. (1960) The effectiveness of tranquilizing drugs plus supportive psychotherapy in treating behaviour disorders of children, *Am. J. Orthopsychiat.* **30**, 113–28.

DALLENBACH, K. (1955) Phrenology versus psychoanalysis, *Am. J. Psychol.* **68**, 511–20.

DAVIDS, A., RYAN, R. and SALVATORE, P. (1968) Effectiveness of residential treatment for psychotic and other disturbed children, *Am. J. Orthopsychiat.* **38**, 469–75.

DAVISON, G. (1968) Systematic desensitization as a counterconditioning process, *J. Abnorm. Psychol.* **73**, 91–99.

DAVISON, G. C. (1969) Appraisal of behaviour modification techniques with adults in institutional settings, in *Behaviour Therapy* (ed. Franks), McGraw-Hill, New York.

DE LEON, E. and MANDELL, W. (1966) A comparison of conditioning and psychotherapy in the treatment of functional enuresis, *J. Clin. Psychol.* **22**, 326–30.

DENKER, P. (1946) Results of treatment of psychoneuroses by the G.P., *N.Y. State J. Med.* **46**, 2164–6.

DICKENSON, W. and TRUAX, C. (1966) Group counselling with college underachievers, *Personnel Guid. J.* **4**, 41–49.

DITTMANN, A. (1966) Psychotherapeutic processes, in *Annual Review of Psychology* (eds. Farnsworth, McNemar and McNemar), Ann. Rev. Inc., Palo Alto.

DONNER, K. and GUERNEY, B. (1969) Automated group desensitization for test anxiety, *Behav. Res. Ther.* **7**, 1–14.

DORFMAN, E. (1958) *Personality Outcomes of Client-centred Child Therapy.* Psychol. Monogr. 72, No. 456.

DUHRSSEN, A. and JORSWIECK, E. (1969) Eine empirisch-statische Untersuchung zur Leistungsfähigkeit. Psychoanalytischer Behandlung, *Berliner Ärztekammer* **12**, 385–9.

DYMOND, R. (1955) Adjustment changes in the absence of psychotherapy, *J. Consult. Psychol.* **19**, 103–7.

EATON, L. and MENOLASCINO, F. (1967) Psychotic reactions of childhood, *Am. J. Orthopsychiat.* **37**, 521–9.

EISENBERG, L. (1957) The course of childhood schizophrenia, *Arch. Neurol. Psychiat.* **78**, 69–83.

EISENBERG, L., CONNERS, K. and SHARPE, L. (1965) A controlled study of the differential application of out-patient psychiatric treatment for children, *Jap. J. Child Psychiat.* **6**, 125–32.

ELLIS, A. (1957) Outcome of employing three techniques of psychotherapy, *J. Clin. Psychol.* **13**, 344–50.

EMERY, J. and KRUMBOLZ, J. (1967) Standard vs. individual hierarchies in desensitization to reduce test anxiety, *J. Counsel. Psychol.* **14**, 204–9.

ENDICOTT, N. and ENDICOTT, J. (1963) "Improvement" in untreated psychiatric patients, *Archs. Gen. Psychiat.* **9**, 575–85.

ENDLER, N. S. (1962) *An S-R Inventory of Anxiousness*, Psychol. Monogr. 76, No. 536.

ENDS, E. and PAGE, C. (1957) A study of 3 types of group psychotherapy with hospitalized male inebriates, *Q. J. Stud. Alcohol.* **18**, 263–77.

ENDS, E. and PAGE, C. (1959) *Group Psychotherapy and Concomitant Psychological Change*, Psychol. Monogr. 73.

ERNST, K. (1959) *Die Prognose der Neurosen*, Springer, Berlin.

EVANS, D. (1970) Exhibitionism, in *Symptoms of Psychopathology* (ed. J. G. Costello), Wiley, New York.

EVANS, I. (1969) Lecture at Maudsley Hospital.

EVANS, I. and NELSON, R. (1968) The combination of learning principles and speech therapy techniques, *J. Child Psychol. Psychiat.* **9**, 111–24.

EYSENCK, H. J. (1952) The effects of psychotherapy: an evaluation, *J. Consult. Psychol.* **16**, 319–24.

EYSENCK, H. J. (1960a) The effects of psychotherapy, in *Handbook of Abnormal Psychology* (ed. H. J. Eysenck), Pitmans, London.

EYSENCK, H. J. (ed.) (1960b) *Behaviour Therapy and the Neuroses*, Pergamon Press, Oxford.

EYSENCK, H. J. (1963) Behaviour therapy, spontaneous remission and transference in neurotics, *Am. J. Psychiat.* **119**, 867–71.

EYSENCK, H. J. (ed.) (1964) *Experiments in Behaviour Therapy*, Pergamon Press, Oxford.

EYSENCK, H. J. (1968) A theory of the incubation of anxiety/fear responses, *Behav. Res. Ther.* **6**, 309–22.

EYSENCK, H. J. (1969a) *The Effects of Psychotherapy*, Science House Inc., New York.

EYSENCK, H. J. (1969b) Relapse and symptom substitution after different types of psychotherapy, *Behav. Res. Ther.* **7**, 283–7.

EYSENCK, H. J. and RACHMAN, S. (1965) *The Causes and Cures of Neuroses*, Routledge & Kegan Paul, London.

FAIRWEATHER, G. *et al.* (1960) *Relative Effectiveness of Psychotherapeutic Programs*, Psychol. Monogr. 74.

FAIRWEATHER, G. and SIMON, R. (1963) A further follow-up comparison of psychotherapeutic programs, *J. Consult. Psychol.* **27**, 186.

FAZIO, A. (1970) Treatment components in implosive therapy, *J. Abnorm. Psychol.* **76**, 106–9.

FEIFEL, H. and EELLS, J. (1963) Patients and therapists assess the same psychotherapy, *J. Consult. Psychol.* **27**, 310–18.

FEIFEL, H. and SCHWARTZ, A. (1953) Group psychotherapy with acutely disturbed psychotic patients, *J. Consult. Psychol.* **17**, 113–21.

FELDMAN, M. P. (1968) The treatment of homosexuality, in *Progress in Behaviour Therapy* (ed. H. Freeman), Wright, Bristol.

FELDMAN, M. P. and MacCULLOCH, M. J. (1965) The application of anticipatory avoidance learning to the treatment of homosexuality: I. Theory, technique, and preliminary results, *Behav. Res. Ther.* **2**, 165–83.

FERSTER, C. B. (1958) Reinforcement and punishment in the control of human behavior by social agencies, *Psychiat. Res. Rep.* **10**, 101–18.

FERSTER, C. B. and DE MEYER, M. (1961) The development of performance in autistic children, *J. Chronic Disorders* **13**, 312–45.

FLEMING, L. and SNYDER, W. (1947) Social and personal changes following non-directive group play therapy, *Am. J. Orthopsychiat.* **17**, 101–16.

FORSYTH, R. and FAIRWEATHER, G. (1961) Psychotherapeutic and other hospital treatment criteria, *J. Abnorm. Soc. Psychol.* **62**, 598–604.

FRANK, J. (1961) *Persuasion and Healing*, Johns Hopkin Press, Baltimore.

FRANK, J. (1968) *The Role of Psychotherapy in Learning* (ed. R. Porter), Churchills, London.

FRANKS, C. (ed.) (1969) *Behaviour Therapy: Appraisal and Status*, McGraw-Hill, New York.

FREUD, S. (1922) *Introductory Lectures on Psychoanalysis*, Allen & Unwin, London.

FREUD, S. (1932) *New Introductory Lectures*, Norton, New York.

FREUD, S. (1940) *An Outline of Psychoanalysis*, Norton, New York.

FRIESS, C. and NELSON, M. J. (1942) Psychoneurotics five years later, *Am. J. Med. Sci.* **203**, 539–58.

GALLAGHER, J. (1953a) Manifest anxiety changes concomitant with client centred therapy, *J. Consult. Psychol.* **17**, 443–6.

GALLAGHER, J. (1953b) MMPI changes concomitant with client centred therapy, *J. Consult. Psychol.* **17**, 334–8.

GARFIELD, Z., DARWIN, P., SINGER, B. and McBREHSTY, J. (1967) Effects of *in vivo* training on experimental desensitization of a phobia, *Psychol. Reports* **20**, 515–19.

GARLINGTON, W. and COTLER, S. (1968) Systematic desensitization of test anxiety, *Behav. Res. Ther.* **6**, 247–56.

GELDER, M., MARKS, I. and WOLFF, H. (1967) Desensitization and psychotherapy in the treatment of phobic states, *Br. J. Psychiat.* **113**, 53–73.

GELLHORN, E. (1964) Motion and emotion, *Psychol. Rev.* **71**, 457–67.

GIEL, R., KNOX, R. and CARSTAIRS, G. (1964) A 5-year follow-up of 100 neurotic outpatients, *Br. Med. J.* **2**, 160–3.

GILLAN, P. (1971) Behaviour therapy and psychotherapy: a comparative investigation. Ph.D. Thesis, London University.

GOLDSTEIN, A. (1960) Patient's expectancies and non-specific therapy as a basis for (un)spontaneous remission, *J. Clin. Psychol.* **18**, 399–403.

GOLDSTEIN, A. (1969) Separate effects of extinction and progressive approach in overcoming fear, *Behav. Res. Ther.* **7**, 47–56.

GRAHAM, S. R. (1960) The effects of psychoanalytically oriented psychotherapy on levels of frequency and satisfaction in sexual activity, *J. Clin. Psychol.* **16**, 94–95.

GREER, H. and CAWLEY, R. (1966) *Some Observations on the Natural History of Neurotic Illness*, Australian Medical Association.

GRINGS, W. and UNO, T. (1968) Counter-conditioning in fear and relaxation, *Psychophysiology* **4**, 479–85.

GRINSPOON, J., EWALT, J. and SHAKER, R. (1968) Psychotherapy and pharmacotherapy in chronic schizophrenia, *Am. J. Psychiat.* **124**, 1645–52.

HAIN, J., BUTCHER, R. and STEVENSON, I. (1966) Systematic desensitization therapy: an analysis of results in 27 patients, *Br. J. Psychiat.* 112, 295–308.

HAMBURG, D. A. (ed.) (1967) *Report of an* ad hoc *Committee on Central Fact-gathering Data* (plus appendices), American Psychoanalytic Association, New York.

HARE, M. (1966) Shortened treatment in a child guidance clinic: the results in 119 cases, *Br. J. Psychiat.* 112, 613–16.

HASLERUD, G., BRADBARD, L., and JOHNSTONE, R. (1954) Cure guidance and handling as components of the Maier technique for breaking fixatives, *J. Psychol.* 37, 27–30.

HASTINGS, D. W. (1958) Follow-up results in psychiatric illness, *Am. J. Psychiat.* 114, 1057–66.

HEILBRUNN, G. (1966) Results with psychoanalytic therapy and professional commitment, *Am. J. Psychother.* 20, 89–99.

HENDERSON, D. and BATCHELOR, I. (1962) Henderson and Gillespie's *Textbook of Psychiatry*, 9th edn., Oxford Univ. Press, London.

HENDERSON, D. and GILLESPIE, R. (1947) *A Textbook of Psychiatry*, 6th edn., Oxford Univ. Press, London.

HENRY, W. and SHLEEN, J. (1958) Affective complexity and psychotherapy, *J Project Tech.* 22, 153–62.

HEWETT, F. (1965) Teaching speech to an autistic child through operant conditioning, *Am. J. Orthopsychiat.* 35, 927–36.

HILL, M. and BLANE, H. T. (1967) Evaluation of psychotherapy with alcoholics: a critical review, *Q. J. Stud. Alcohol.* 28, 76–104.

HINDE, R. (1968) *The Role of Learning in Psychotherapy* (ed. R. Porter), Churchill, London.

HINGTEN, J., COULTER, S. and CHURCHILL, D. (1967) Intensive reinforcement of imitative behaviour in mute autistic children, *Archs. Gen. Psychiat.* 17, 36–43.

HOGAN, R. (1968) The implosive technique, *Behav. Res. Ther.* 6, 423–32.

HOGAN, R. and KIRCHNER, J. (1967) A preliminary report of the extinction of learned fears via short-term implosive therapy, *J. Abnorm. Psychol.* 72, 106–9.

HOGAN, R. and KIRCHNER, J. (1968) Implosive, eclectic verbal, and bibliotherapy in the treatment of fears of snakes, *Behav. Res. Ther.* 6, 167–72.

HOLLINGSHEAD, A. and REDLICH, F. (1958) *Social Class and Mental Illness*, Wiley, New York.

HOLMES, F. (1938) *An Experimental Study of Fear in Young Children*, Child Devel. Monogr. No. 20.

HORWITZ, W., POLATIN, P., KOLB, L. and HOCH, P. (1958) A study of cases of schizophrenia treated by "direct analysis", *Am. J. Psychiat.* 114, 870–3.

HUMPHERY, J. (1966) Behaviour therapy with children: an experimental evaluation, Ph.D. thesis, Univ. of London.

HUSSAIN, A. (1964) Behaviour therapy using hypnosis, in *The Conditioning Therapies* (eds. Wolpe, Salter, and Reyna), Holt, Rinehart & Winston, New York.

IMBER, S., FRANK, J., NASH, E. and GLEIDMAN, L. (1957) Improvement and amount of therapeutic contact, *J. Consult. Psychol.* 77, 283–393.

IMBER, S., NASH, E., HOEHN-SARIC, R., STONE, A. and FRANK, J. L. (1968) A 10-year follow-up of treated psychiatric outpatients, in *An Evaluation of the Results of the Psychotherapies* (ed. Lesse), Thomas, Springfield.

ISAACS, W., THOMAS, J. and GOLDIAMOND, I. (1960) Application of operant conditioning, *J. Speech Hearing Dis.* **25**, 842–52.

JENSEN, G. and WOMACK, M. (1967) Operant conditioning techniques applied in the treatment of an autistic child, *Am. J. Orthopsychiat.* **37**, 30–34.

JOHNSON, S. and SECHREST, L. (1968) Comparison of desensitization and progressive relaxation in treating test anxiety, *J. Consult. Clin. Psychol.* **32**, 280–6.

JURJEVICH, R. M. (1968) Changes in psychiatric symptoms without psychotherapy, in *An Evaluation of the Results of the Psychotherapies* (ed. Lesse), Thomas, Springfield.

KAHN, M. and BAKER, B. (1968) Desensitization with minimal therapist contact, *J. Abnorm. Psychol.* **73**, 198–200.

KALINOWSKY, L. (1967) Insulin coma treatment, in *Comprehensive Textbook of Psychiatry* (eds. A. Freedman and H. Kaplan), Williams, Wilkins, Baltimore.

KALINOWSKY, L. and HOCH, P. (1952) *Shock Treatments and Psychosurgery in Psychiatry*, 2nd edn., Grune & Stratton, New York.

KATAHN, M., STRENGER, S., and CHERRY, N. (1966) Group counselling and behaviour therapy with test-anxious college students, *J. Consult. Psychol.* **30**, 544–9.

KEDWARD, H. (1969) The outcome of neurotic illness in the community, *Social Psychiat.* **4**, 1–4.

KELLNER, R. (1967) The evidence in favour of psychotherapy, *Br. J. Med. Psychol.* **40**, 341–58.

KENNEDY, T. (1964) Treatment of chronic schizophrenia by behavior therapy, *Behav. Res. Ther.* **2**, 1–6.

KERR, N., MEYERSON, L., and MICHAEL, J. (1965) A procedure for shaping vocalization in a mute child, in *Case Studies in Behaviour Modification* (eds. L. Ullmann and L. Krasner), Holt, Rinehart, & Winston, New York.

KIESLER, D. (1966) Some myths of psychotherapy, *Psychol. Bull.* **65**, 110–36.

KIND, H. (1969) Prognosis, in *The Schizophrenic Syndrome* (eds. L. Bellak and L. Loeb), Grune & Stratton, New York.

KLEIN, H. (1960) A study of changes occurring in patients during and after psychoanalytic treatment, in *Current Approaches to Psychoanalysis* (eds. P. Hoch and J. Zubin), Grune & Stratton, New York.

KNAPP, P., LEVIN, S., McCARTER, R., WERNER, H. and ZETZEL, E. (1960) Suitability for psychoanalysis: a review of 100 supervised analytic cases, *Psychoanal. Q.* **29**, 459–77.

KNIGHT, R. P. (1941) Evaluation of the results of psychoanalytic therapy, *Am. J. Psychiat.* **98**, 434–46.

KOEGLER, R. and BRILL, N. (1967) *Treatment of Psychiatric Outpatients*, Appleton-Century-Crofts, New York.

KONDAS, O. (1967) Reduction of examination anxiety and "stage fright" by group desensitization and relaxation, *Behav. Res. Ther.* **5**, 275–82.

KRASNER, L. (1962) The therapist as a social reinforcement machine, in *Research in Psychotherapy*, American Psychoanalytic Association, New York.

KRASNER, L. (1968) Discussion, in *Ciba Symposium* (ed. R. Porter), p. 326.

KRASNER, L. (1970) The behavior modification approach in the helping professions, in *Progress in Behavior Modification* (ed. J. Nagoshi), Univ. of Hawaii Press.

KRAUS, A. R. (1959) Experimental study of the effect of group psychotherapy with chronic schizophrenic patients, *Int. J. Group Psychother.* **9**, 293–302.

KRINGLEN, E. (1965) Obsessional neurosis: a long-term follow-up, *Br. J. Psychiat.* **111**, 709–14.

LADER, M. and MATHEWS, A. (1968) A physiological model of phobic anxiety and desensitization, *Behav. Res. Ther.* **6**, 411–21.

LADER, M. and WING, L. (1966) *Physiological Measures, Sedative Drugs, and Morbid Anxiety*, Maudsley Monogr., No. 14.

LANDIS, C. (1937) A statistical evaluation of psychotherapeutic methods, in *Concepts and Problems in Psychotherapy* (ed. L. E. Hinsie), Columbi. Univ. Press, New York.

LANG, P. (1969) *Behaviour Therapy: Appraisal and Status* (ed. C. Franks), McGraw-Hill, New York.

LANG, P. and LAZOVIK, A. (1963) The experimental desensitization of a phobia, *J. Abnorm. Soc. Psychol.* **66**, 519–25.

LANG, P., LAZOVIK, A. and REYNOLDS, D. (1966) Desensitization, suggestibility, and pseudo-therapy, *J. Abnorm. Psychol.* **70**, 395–402.

LANYON, R., MANOSEVITZ, M. and IMBER, R. L. (1968) Systematic desensitization: distribution of practice, *Behav. Res. Ther.* **6**, 323–30.

LAZARUS, A. A. (1961) Group therapy of phobic disorders, *J. Abnorm. Soc. Psychol.* **63**, 504–12.

LAZARUS, A. A. (1963) The results of behaviour therapy in 126 cases of severe neurosis, *Behav. Res. Ther.* **1**, 65–78b.

LESSE, S. (ed.) (1968) *An Evaluation of the Results of the Psychotherapies*, Thomas, Springfield.

LEVIS, D. and CARRERA, R. (1967) The effects of 10 hours of implosive therapy in the treatment of outpatients, *J. Abnorm. Psychol.* **72**, 504–8.

LEVITT, E. E. (1957) A comparison of "remainers" and "defectors" among child clinic patients, *J. Consult. Psychol.* **21**, 316.

LEVITT, E. (1963) Psychotherapy with children: a further evaluation, *Behav. Res. Ther.* **1**, 45–51.

LEVITT, E., BEISER, H. and ROBERTSON, R. (1959) A follow-up evaluation of cases treated at a community child guidance clinic, *Am. J. Orthopsychiat.* **29**, 337–45.

LINDELIUS, R. (ed.) (1970) A study of schizophrenia, *Acta Psychiat. Scandin.*, Suppl. 216.

LINDSLEY, O. (1956) Operant conditioning methods applied to research in chronic schizophrenia, *Psychiat. Res. Rep.* **5**, 118–39.

LINDSLEY, O. (1960) Characteristics of the behaviour of chronic psychotics, *Dis. Nerv. System* **2**, 66–78.

LOMONT, J. F. (1965) Reciprocal inhibition or extinction?, *Behav. Res. Ther.* **3**, 209–20.

LOMONT, J. F. and EDWARDS, J. E. (1967) The role of relaxation in systematic desensitization, *Behav. Res. Ther.* **5**, 11–26.

LORR, M., McNAIR, D., MICHAUX, W. and RASKIN, A. L. (1962) Frequency of treatment and change in psychotherapy, *J. Abnorm. Soc. Psychol.* **64**, 281–92.

LOVAAS, I. (1966) A program for the establishment of speech in psychotic children, in *Childhood Autism* (ed. J. Wing), Pergamon Press, Oxford.

LOVIBOND, S. H. and COOTE, M. (1970) Enuresis, in *Symptoms of Psychopathology* (ed. C. G. Costello), Wiley, New York.

LOWE, C. (1961) The self-concept: fact or artifact?, *Psychol. Bull.* **58**, 325–36.

172   BIBLIOGRAPHY

MacCulloch, M., Feldman, M. P., Orford, J. and MacCulloch, M. L. (1966) Anticipatory avoidance learning in the treatment of alcoholism: a record of therapeutic failure, *Behav. Res. Ther.* 4, 187–96.

MacFarlane, J. W., Allen, L., and Honzik, M. (1954) *A Developmental Study of the Behavior Problems of Normal Children*, Univ. of Calif. Press, Berkeley.

McCance, C. and McCance, P. (1969) Alcoholism in north-east Scotland: its treatment and outcome, *Br. J. Psychiat.* 115, 189–98.

McGlynn, F. and Mapp, R. (1970) Systematic desensitization of snake avoidance following 3 types of suggestion, *Behav. Res. Ther.* 8, 197–201.

McGuire, R. and Vallance, M. (1964) Aversion therapy by electric shock: a simple technique, *Br. Med. J.* 1, 151–2.

Malan, D., Bacal, H., Heath, E. and Balfour, F. L. (1968) A study of psychodynamic changes in untreated neurotic patients, *Br. J. Psychiat.* 114, 525–51.

Malleson, N. (1959) Panic and phobia, *Lancet* 1, 225–7.

Mann, J. and Rosenthal, T. (1969) Vicarious and direct counterconditioning of test anxiety, *Behav. Res. Ther.* 7, 359–68.

Marks, I. M. (1969) *Fears and Phobias*, Heinemann, London.

Marks, I. M. and Gelder, M. G. (1965) A controlled retrospective study of behaviour therapy in phobic patients, *Br. J. Psychiat.* 111, 561–73.

Marks, I. M. and Gelder, M. G. (1966a) Severe agoraphobia: a controlled prospective trial of behaviour therapy, *Br. J. Psychiat.* 112, 309–20.

Marks, I. M. and Gelder, M. G. (1966b) Different ages of onset in varieties of phobia, *Am. J. Psychiat.* 123, 218–21.

Marks, I. M. and Gelder, M. G. (1967) Transvestism and fetishism: clinical and psychological changes during faradic aversion, *Br. J. Psychiat.* 119, 711–30.

Marks, I. M., Gelder, M. G. and Bancroft, J. (1970) Sexual deviants two years after electrical aversion, *Br. J. Psychiat.* 17, 173–85.

Marks, J., Schalock, R., and Sonoda, B. (1967) Reinforcement versus relationship therapy for schizophrenics, *Proc. Am. Psychiat. Ass.* 237–8.

Masserman, J. H. (1943) *Behavior and Neurosis*, Chicago Univ. Press, Chicago.

Masserman, J. H. (1955) *The Practice of Dynamic Psychiatry*, Saunders, New York.

Massimo, J. and Shore, M. (1963) The effectiveness of a comprehensive vocationally oriented psychotherapeutic program for delinquent boys, *Am. J. Orthopsychiat.* 33, 634–42.

Masterson, J. (1967) The symptomatic adolescent 5 years later, *Am. J. Psychiat.* 123, 1338–45.

Mathews, A. (1971) Psychophysiology and behaviour therapy, *Psychol. Bulletin.* (In press.)

May, P. and Tuma, A. H. (1965) Treatment of schizophrenia, *Br. J. Psychiat.* 111, 503–10.

Mayer-Gross, W., Slater, E. and Roth, M. (1960) *Clinical Psychiatry*, 2nd edn., Cassell, London.

Mealia, W. (1968) The comparative effectiveness of systematic desensitization and implosive therapy, Ph.D. dissert., Univ. Missouri.

Meehl, P. (1955) Psychotherapy, *Ann. Rev. Psychol.* 6, 357–78.

Melamed, B. and Lang, P. (1967) Study of the automated desensitization of fear, *Conference of the Midwestern Psychological Association, Chicago*.

Meyer, V. (1967) Modification of expectations in cases with obsessional rituals, *Behav. Res. Ther.* 4, 273–80.

MEYER, V. and CRISP, A. H. (1966) Some problems of behaviour therapy, *Br. J. Psychiat.* **112**, 367–82.

MEYER, V. and GELDER, M. G. (1963) Behaviour therapy and complex disorders, *Br. J. Psychiat.* **109**, 19–28.

MILLER, H. and NAWAS, M. (1970) The comparative effectiveness of pairing aversive imagery with relaxation, neutral tasks, and muscular tension in reducing snake phobia, *Behav. Res. Ther.* **8**, 63–68.

MITCHELL, K. and INGHAM, R. (1970) The effects of general anxiety on group desensitization of test anxiety, *Behav. Res. Ther.* **8**, 69–78.

MONROE, J. and HILL, H. (1958) The Hill–Monroe inventory for predicting acceptability for psychotherapy in the institutionalized narcotic addict, *J. Clin. Psychol.* **14**, 31–36.

MOORE, N. (1965) Behaviour therapy in bronchial asthma: a controlled study, *J. Psychosomatic Res.* **9**, 257–74.

MOOS, R. and CLEMES, S. (1967) Multivariate study of the patient–therapist system, *J. Consult. Psychol.* **31**, 119–30.

MORRIS, H., ESCOLL, P. and WEXTER, R. (1955) Aggressive behavior disorders of childhood, *Am. J. Psychiat.* **112**, 991–7.

MORRIS, D., SOROKER, E., and BURNS, M. (1954) Follow-up studies of shy, withdrawn children, *Am. J. Ortho.* **24**, 743–54.

MOWBRAY, R. and TIMBURY, G. (1966) Opinions on psychotherapy, *Br. J. Psychiat.* **112**, 351–61.

MUEHLBERG, N., PIERCE, R., and DRASGOW, J. (1969) A factor analysis of therapeutically facilitative conditions, *J. Clin. Psychol.* **25**, 93–95.

MURRAY, E. J. (1962) Paper read at Am. Psychoanal. Ass. Conv., St. Louis, quoted by Costello, C. G. (1963).

MYERSON, A. (1939) Theory and principles of the "total push" method in the treatment of chronic schizophrenia, *Am. J. Psychiat.* **95**, 1197–1204.

NAWAS, M., FISHMAN, S. and PURCEL, J. (1970) A standardized desensitization program, *Behav. Res. Ther.* **8**, 49–56.

NEWMAN, L. and STOLLER, R. (1969) Spider symbolism and bisexuality, *J. Am. Psychoanal. Ass.* **17**, 862–72.

OBLER, M. and TERWILLIGER, R. (1970) Pilot study on the effectiveness of systematic desensitization with neurologically impaired children with phobic disorders, *J. Consult. Clin. Psychol.* **34**, 314–18.

O'CONNOR, J., DANIELS, G., KARSH, A., MOSES, L., FLOOD, C. and STERN, L. (1964) The effects of psychotherapy on the course of ulcerative colitis, *Am. J. Psychiat.* **120**, 738–42.

O'DONNELL, J. (1965) The relapse rate in narcotics addiction, in *Narcotics* (eds. D. Wilner and R. Kassebaum), McGraw-Hill, New York.

OLIVEAU, D., AGRAS, W., LEITENBERG, H., MOORE, R. and WRIGHT, D. (1969) Systematic desensitization, instructions, and positive reinforcement, *Behav. Res. Ther.* **7**, 27–35.

O'NEAL, P. and ROBINS, L. (1958) The relation of childhood disorders to adult psychiatric status, *Am. J. Psychiat.* **114**, 961–9.

O'NEILL, D. and HOWELL, J. (1969) Three modes of hierarchy presentation in systematic desensitization, *Behav. Res. Ther.* **7**, 289–94.

ORGEL, S. (1958) Effects of psychoanalysis on the course of peptic ulcer, *Psychosomatic Med.* **20**, 117–25.

Passingham, R. (1970) Personal communication.

Paul, G. (1966) *Insight versus Desensitization in Psychotherapy*, Stanford Univ. Press, Stanford.

Paul, G. and Shannon, D. (1966) Treatment of anxiety through systematic desensitization in therapy groups, *J. Abnorm. Psychol.* **71**, 124–35.

Phillips, E. L. (1957) *Psychotherapy: A Modern Theory and Practice*, Staples, London.

Phillips, E. L., Raiford, A. and El-Batrawi, S. (1965) The Q-sort re-evaluated, *J. Consult. Psychol.* **29**, 422–5.

Polin, A. (1959) The effect of flooding and physical suppression as extinction techniques on an anxiety-motivated avoidance response, *J. Psychol.* **47**, 253–5.

Porter, R. (ed.) (1968) *The Role of Learning in Psychotherapy*, Ciba Symposium, Churchills, London.

Powdermaker, F. and Frank, J. (1953) *Group Psychotherapy*, Harvard Univ. Press, Cambridge.

Powers, E. and Witmer, H. (1951) *An Experiment on the Prevention of Delinquency*, Columbia Univ. Press, New York.

Proctor, S. (1969) Duration of exposure of items and pre-treatment training as factors in systematic desensitization therapy, in *Advances in Behaviour Therapy*, 1968 (eds. R. Rubin and C. Franks), Academic Press, New York.

Psychrembel, W. (1964) *Klinisches Wörterbuch*, Berlin, Gruyter.

Rachman, S. (ed.) (1963) *Critical Essays on Psychoanalysis*, Pergamon Press, Oxford.

Rachman, S. (1965) Studies in desensitization: I, The separate effects of relaxation and desensitization, *Behav. Res. Ther.* **3**, 245–52.

Rachman, S. (1966) Studies in desensitization: III, Flooding, *Behav. Res. Ther.* **4**, 1–6.

Rachman, S. (1967) Systematic desensitization, *Psychol. Bull.* **67**, 93–103.

Rachman, S. (1968) *Phobias—Their Nature and Control*, Thomas, Springfield.

Rachman, S. (1969) *Verhaltenstherapie bei Phobien* (trans. J. Bergold), Urban & Schwarzenberg, Munich.

Rachman, S. and Teasdale, J. (1969) *Aversion Therapy and Behaviour Disorders*, Routledge & Kegan Paul, London.

Ramsay, R. W., Barends, J., Breuker, J. and Kruseman, A. (1966) Massed versus spaced desensitization of fear, *Behav. Res. Ther.* **4**, 205–8.

Report of the British Psycho-Analytical Society, 1967.

Ricks, D. *et al.* (1964) A measure of increased temporal perspective in successfully treated delinquent boys, *J. Abnorm. Soc. Psychol.* **69**, 685–9.

Risley, T. and Wolf, M. (1967) Establishing functional speech in echolalic children, *Behav. Res. Ther.* **5**, 73–88.

Ritter, B. (1968) Group desensitization of children's snake phobias, *Behav. Res. Ther.* **6**, 1–6.

Robertson, J. (1961) Effects of different rewards on modifying schizophrenics, *J. Clin. Psychol.* **7**, 399–402.

Robinson, C. and Suinn, R. (1969) Group desensitization of a phobia in a massed session, *Behav. Res. Ther.* **7**, 319–22.

Rogers, C. R. (1957) The necessary and sufficient conditions of therapeutic personality change, *J. Consult. Psychol.* **21**, 95–103.

Rogers, C. R. and Dymond, R. (1954) *Psychotherapy and Personality Change*, Chicago Univ. Press, Chicago.

ROGERS, C. R., GENDLIN, E., KIESLER, D. and TRUAX, C. (1967) *The Therapeutic Relationship and its Impact: a Study of Psychotherapy with Schizophrenics*, Wisconsin Univ. Press, Madison.

ROSEN, J. (1953) *Direct Analysis*, Grune & Stratton, New York.

ROSENTHAL, D. (1962) Book review, *Psychiatry* 25, 377–80.

ROSENZWEIG, S. (1954) A transvaluation of psychotherapy: a reply to Eysenck, *J. Abnorm. Soc. Psychol.* 49, 298–304.

RUTTER, M. (1965) The influence of organic and emotional factors on the origins, nature, and outcome of childhood psychosis, *Develop. Med. Child. Neurol.* 7, 518–28.

RUTTER, M. (Ed.) (1971) *Infantile Autism*, Churchills, London.

SACKS, J. and BERGER, S. (1954) Group therapy with hospitalized chronic schizophrenic patients, *J. Consult. Psychol.* 18, 297–302.

SAENGER, G. (1970) Patterns of change among treated and untreated patients seen in psychiatric community mental health clinics, *J. Nerv. Ment. Dis.* 150, 37–50.

SALZINGER, K., FELDMAN, R., COWAN, J., and SALZINGER, S. L. (1965) Operant conditioning of verbal behaviour in two speech-deficient boys, in *Research in Behaviour Modification* (eds. L. Krasner and L. Ullmann), Holt, Rinehart & Winston, New York.

SANFORD, N. (1953) Psychotherapy, *Ann. Rev. Psychol.* 4, 317–42.

SARGANT, W. (1959) Insulin treatment in England, in *Insulin Treatment in Psychiatry* (eds. M. Rinkel and H. Himwich), Philos. Library, Inc., New York.

SASLOW, G. and PETERS, A. (1956) Follow-up of "untreated" patients with behaviour disorders, *Psychiatric. Q.* 30, 283–302.

SATZ, P. and BARAFF, A. (1962) Changes in relations between self-concepts and ideal-concepts of psychotics consequent upon therapy, *J. Gen. Psychol.* 67, 291–8.

SCHEFLEN, A. (1961) *A Psychotherapy of Schizophrenia*, Thomas, Springfield.

SCHELL, R., STARK, R. and GIDDAN, L. (1967) Development of language behaviour in an autistic child, *J. Speech Hearing Dis.* 32, 51–64.

SCHMIDT, E., CASTELL, D. and BROWN, P. (1965) A retrospective study of 42 cases of behaviour therapy, *Behav. Res. Ther.* 3, 9–20.

SCHORER, C., LOWINGER, P., SULLIVAN, T. and HARTLAUB, G. (1968) Improvement without treatment, *Dis. Nerv. System* 29, 100–4.

SEEMAN, J. and EDWARDS, B. (1954) A therapeutic approach to reading difficulties, *J. Consult. Psychol.* 18, 451–3.

SEMON, R. and GOLDSTEIN, N. (1957) The effectiveness of group psychotherapy with chronic schizophrenic patients, *J. Consult. Psychol.* 21, 317–22.

SHAPIRO, D. (1969) Empathy, warmth, and genuineness in psychotherapy, *Br. J. Soc. Clin. Psychol.* 8, 350–61.

SHEPHERD, M. and GRUENBERG, E. (1957) The age for neuroses, *Millbank Memor., Q. Bull.* 35, 258–65.

SHEPHERD, M., OPENNHEIM, A. and MITCHELL, S. (1966) Childhood behaviour disorders and the child guidance clinic: an epidemiological study, *J. Child. Psychol. Psychiat.* 7, 39–52.

SHLIEN, J., MOSAK, H., and DREIKURS, R. (1962) Effect of time limits: a comparison of two psychotherapies, *J. Counsel. Psychol.* 9, 31–34.

SHORE, M. and MASSIMO, J. (1966) Comprehensive vocationally oriented psychotherapy for adolescent boys: a follow-up study, *Am. J. Orthopsychiat.* 36, 609–15.

SIDMAN, M. (1960) *Tactics of Scientific Research*, Basic Books, New York.

SKINNER, B. F. (1957) *Verbal Behavior*, Appleton, New York.

SKINNER, B. F. (1959) *Cumulative Record*, Appleton, New York.

SLATER, E. (1970) Psychiatry: science and non-science, 3rd Mapother Lecture, Inst. of Psychiatry, London.

SLATER, E. and ROTH, M. (1969) *Clinical Psychiatry*, (3rd edn.), Baillière, London.

SLOANE, H., JOHNSTON, M. and HARRIS, F. (1968) Remedial procedures for teaching verbal behaviour to speech deficients, in *Operant Procedures in Remedial Speech and Language Training* (eds. H. Sloane and B. Macaulay), Houghton Mifflin Inc., Boston.

STAMPFL, T. (1967) Implosive therapy, in *Behaviour Modification Techniques in the Treatment of Emotional Disorders* (ed. S. Armtage), V.A. Publ., Michigan.

STAMPFL, T. and LEVIS, D. (1967) Essentials of implosive therapy, *J. Abnorm. Psychol.* **72**, 496–503.

STAMPFL, T. and LEVIS, D. (1968) Implosive therapy—a behavioural therapy?, *Behav. Res. Ther.* **6**, 31–36.

STEVENSON, I. (1961) Processes of "spontaneous" recovery from the psychoneuroses, *Am. J. Psychiat.* **117**, 1057–64.

STRUPP, H. and BERGIN, A. (1969) Some empirical and conceptual bases for co-ordinated research in psychotherapy, *Int. J. Psychiat.* **7**, 18–90.

SUINN, R. (1968) The desensitization of test anxiety by group and individual therapy, *Behav. Res. Ther.* **6**, 385–8.

TAYLOR, D. (1955) Changes in the self-concept without psychotherapy, *J. Consult. Psychol.* **19**, 205–9.

TEASDALE, J. (1969) Research in psychotherapy, unpublished MS.

TEUBER, N. and POWERS, E. (1953) Evaluating therapy in a delinquency prevention program, *Proc. Ass. Nerv. Ment. Dis.* **3**, 138–47.

THOMAS, A., CHESS, S., and BIRCH, H. (1968) *Temperament and Behaviour Disorders in Children*, New York Univ. Press, New York.

TRUAX, C. and CARKHUFF, R. (1967) *Toward Effective Counselling and Psychotherapy*, Aldine Press, Chicago.

TRUAX, C., FINE, H., MORAVEC, J., and MILLIS, W. (1968) Effects of therapist persuasive potency in individual psychotherapy, *J. Clin. Psychol.* **24**, 359–65.

TRUAX, C., FRANK, I., and IMBER, S. (1966) Therapist empathy, genuineness, and warmth and patient outcome, *J. Consult. Psychol.* **30**, 395–401.

TURNER, R., YOUNG, G., and RACHMAN, S. (1970) Treatment of nocturnal enuresis, *Behav. Res. Ther.* **8**, 367–82.

ULLMANN, L. and KRASNER, L. (1965) *Case Studies in Behaviour Modification*, Holt, Rinehart & Winston, New York.

VOGLER, R., LUNDE, S., JOHNSON, G., and MARTIN, P. (1970) Electrical aversion conditioning with chronic alcoholics, *J. Consult. Clin. Psychol.* **34**, 302–7.

VORSTER, D. (1966) Psychotherapy and the results of psychotherapy, *S. African Med. J.* **40**, 934–6.

WAGNER, M. and CAUTHEN, N. (1968) A comparison of operant conditioning and reciprocal inhibition in systematic desensitization, *Behav. Res. Ther.* **6**, 225–7.

WALLACE, H. and WHYTE, M. (1959) Natural history of the psychoneuroses, *Br. Med. J.* **1**, 144–8.

WARREN, W. (1965) A study of adolescent psychiatric in-patients: II, The follow-up study, *J. Child Psychol. Psychiat.* **6**, 141–60.

WEISS, H. and BORN, B. (1967) Speech training or language acquisition?, *Am. J. Orthopsychiat.* 37, 49–55.

WERRY, J. and COHRSSEN, J. (1965) Enuresis—an aetiologic and therapeutic study, *J. Pediatrics* 67, 423–31.

WERRY, J. and SPRAGUE, R. (1970) Hyperactivity, in *Symptoms of Psychopathology* (ed. C. G. Costello), Wiley, New York.

WESTWOOD, G. (1960) *A Minority*, Longmans, London.

WETZEL, R., BAKER, J., RONEY, M. and MARTIN, M. (1966) Outpatient treatment of autistic behaviour, *Behav. Res. Ther.* 4, 169–77.

WILLIS, J. and BANNISTER, D. (1965) The diagnosis and treatment of schizophrenia, *Br. J. Psychiat.* 111, 1165–71.

WILLIS, R. and EDWARDS, J. (1969) A study of the comparative effectiveness of desensitization and implosion, *Behav. Res. Ther.* 7, 387–96.

WILSON, F. and WALTERS, T. (1966) Modification of speech output in near-mute schizophrenics, *Behav. Res. Ther.* 4, 59–67.

WING, J. K. (1966) Five-year outcome in early schizophrenia, *Proc. Roy. Soc. Med.* 59, 17–18.

WING, J. K. (1968) Social treatments of mental illness, in *Studies in Psychiatry* (eds. M. Shepherd and D. Davies), Oxford Univ. Press, Oxford.

WING, J. and FREUDENBERG, R. (1961) The response of severely ill chronic schizophrenic patients to social stimulation, *Am. J. Psychiat.* 118, 311–22.

WITTENBORN, J. (1961) Contributions and current state of Q-methodology, *Psychol. Bull.* 58, 132–42.

WOLF, M., RISLEY, T. and MEES, H. (1964) Application of operant conditioning to an autistic child, *Behav. Res. Ther.* 1, 305–12.

WOLPE, J. (1958) *Psychotherapy by Reciprocal Inhibition*, Stanford Univ. Press, Stanford.

WOLPE, J. (1963) Behaviour therapy in complex neurotic states. Paper read at Reading Conference of British Psychological Society.

WOLPE, J. (1964) The comparative status of conditioning therapy and psychoanalysis, in *The Conditioning Therapies* (ed. J. Wolpe), Holt, Rinehart & Winston, New York.

WOLPE, J. and RACHMAN, S. (1960) Psychoanalytic evidence: a critique based on Freud's case of Little Hans, *J. Nerv. Ment. Dis.* 131, 135–45.

WYLIE, R. (1961) *The Self Concept*, Univ. Nebraska Press, Nebraska.

ZEISSET, R. (1968) Desensitization and relaxation in the modification of psychiatric patients' interview behaviour, *J. Abnorm. Psychol.* 73, 18–24.

ZUBIN, J. (1953) Evaluation of therapeutic outcome in mental disorders, *J. Nerv. Ment. Dis.* 117, 95–111.

NAME INDEX

Abraham 123
Adams, H. 155
Anderson, O. 142
Anker, J. 113, 114
Ashcraft, C. 66
Atthowe, J. 149
Auerbach, A. 107
Ayllon, T. 149, 156
Azima, H. 116
Azrin, N. 149, 156

Baehr, G. 88
Baker, B. 126, 128
Bancroft, J. 146
Bandura, A. 121, 124, 128, 129, 132, 149, 157
Bannister, D. 3, 108
Baraff, A. 112
Barbour, R. F. 100
Barendregt, J. T. 51, 62
Barrett, C. 127
Barron, F. 11, 12, 65, 70, 86
Beebe, G. 12
Beedell, C. J. 100
Bellak, L. 107
Bendig, A. 36
Bennet, I. 1
Bentler, P. M. 142
Berger, S. 115
Bergin, A. E. 16, 27–40, 42, 44, 46, 64, 65, 84, 85, 86, 87, 88
Bieber, I. 47
Bills 68
Birnbrauer, J. 149
Blake, B. G. 147
Blake, P. 155
Born, B. 154

Boulougouris, J. 128
Boyer, L. 107
Brawley, E. 155
Brill, A. A. 110
Brill, N. 4, 12, 29, 40, 52, 78, 80, 81
Brody, M. 44, 46, 48
Bucher, B. 149, 153
Burnett, A. 135

Cappon, D. 29, 30, 31
Carkhuff, R. 16, 90, 91, 94, 95
Cartwright, D. S. 24, 25, 86
Cartwright, R. D. 94
Cauthen, N. 129
Cawley, R. 19, 20, 21, 81, 82, 83
Chess, S. 105
Clark, D. F. 143
Clein, L. 97
Clemes, S. 94
Cohen, R. 126, 149
Cohrssen, J. 103
Collingwood, T. 93
Cook, C. 155
Cooke, G. 125
Coombs, A. 88
Cooper, J. E. 109, 135, 136, 137, 141
Coote, M. 103
Costello, C. G. 141
Cotler, S. 126, 127
Cowden, R. 112
Cowen, E. 88
Creak, E. 99
Cremerius, J. 26, 27, 55, 56, 57, 59
Crighton, J. 126
Crisp, A. H. 138, 140, 141
Cross, H. J. 64, 65
Crossman, R. 121

179

SUBJECT INDEX

OTHER TITLES IN THE SERIES IN EXPERIMENTAL PSYCHOLOGY